MESSAGING

MESSAGING

A Spiritual Path toward Healing from Grief

The Art and Mastery of Self Healing
through your Inner Voice of Spirit

An Awakening to Self Transformation through a Fifteen Day Process
of Writing, Emotional Awareness, and Soul Exploration

By **DEBRA ANN** - Emotional Intelligence Life Coach
This book also includes **Heavenly Messages~ Forever In My Heart®** poems written by Debra Ann. They are her unique brand of messages that offer words to the silence of grief. These messages are published as spiritual eternity cards. They were inspired by the memory and written in honor of all who are no longer with us but who remain in our hearts forever.

iUniverse, Inc.
Bloomington

Messaging
A Spiritual Path toward Healing from Grief

iUniverse books may be ordered through booksellers or by contacting:

iUniverse
1663 Liberty Drive
Bloomington, IN 47403
www.iuniverse.com
1-800-Authors (1-800-288-4677)

ISBN: 978-1-4502-3848-9 (sc)
ISBN: 978-1-4502-3849-6 (ebk)

Printed in the United States of America

iUniverse rev. date: 02/25/2011

Foreword

This book you are holding in your hands will introduce you to a powerful tool for self healing called Messaging. It is a writing activity that serves as a cleansing process and a purification of the soul. Through Messaging, the spirit pushes out all the toxic waste that has been improperly filtered through your life, especially through the grief experience. These toxins have clogged the transmission of the eternal love that is waiting to drench and cleanse your heart. You will discover inner spirit, divine vision, and your unlimited capacity to love beyond this physical dimension by understanding yourself and others with compassion.

Jesus told a parable in Luke 5:37, which says, "And no one pours new wine into old wineskins; if he does, the fresh wine will burst the skins and it will be spilled and the skins will be ruined (destroyed)." This means you need to cleanse and purify your soul in order for your heart to connect and be filled with the healing power of eternal truth. Through prayer, meditation, visualization, affirmations and the process of Messaging, you will embark on the spiritual path toward healing from grief.

Messaging is a writing process that came through me as I was beginning to heal from an intense period of grief and loss in my life. Life often speaks to us during difficult times. Most of us are so deafened by the suffering that we cannot hear the quiet voice that is aching to break out. It is when we are struggling that we need to ask life what it would like to express through us. It is in the careful listening and creative expression through the darkness of life that we will find a light to heal. When God is trying to move pain through you and create something from you, it usually happens when you are alone and in the dark. This is the natural process of life from conception through birth.

Your willingness to listen to the quiet voice within you right now will allow God to give birth to new life from the pain. The Messaging Process allows your heart to experience every challenge in life with openness. Through Messaging, you discover that you are not alone in your grief or whatever hurt you are facing in life. Through this creative writing process, you discover that we are all one. We are one in the collective consciousness of all beings through eternity. When you see yourself in the oneness of your truth, you begin to understand and accept the importance of healing. The Messaging Process allows you to confront your emotions and get your mind off of your own suffering.

Through Messaging, healing comes to you by listening to your emotions as a source of information and also by connecting you to the heart of every other person who is experiencing the same hurt as you. It doesn't matter if you are young or old or if you are experiencing a recent loss or a loss from the past, this process will guide toward healing. All you need are a willing heart and the ability to read and write and you are on your way. When you begin to listen to your heart, to understand your emotions, and feel yourself through another, true healing can begin to manifest because you are listening to the eternal eloquence of spirit.

Throughout my own healing process, I began a search for truth and meaning so that I could find a way to put together the broken pieces in my life. If I were to tell you that I found the answers to the mysteries in life, such as death, I would be lying. But I can tell you that I have found an internal knowing to the divine mystical presence in every mystery. And with this I have discovered a peaceful contentment with life and all its changes.

For many years, I have had an interest and have actually lived my life with an understanding from various topics in spirituality, metaphysics, philosophy, and psychology. The knowing and application of these thoughts have allowed me to embrace the momentary movement and healing through grief. Although grief is one of life's most difficult experiences, it is also life's most transformational. I could go into the pain and agony of my own grief experience, but I choose not to write from darkness when the light offers more clarity and peace. The truth is, it is not important for you to know my grief experience, and it isn't necessary that I know yours. We know what has brought us here together today. You can choose right now, with me, spirit and every hurting heart in consciousness at your side, to release yourself from your grief story too.

You can choose not to define your loved one's life and your life today by the memory of death. You can choose another story—the story of truth which honors life. These are the infinite tales of wisdom that grief attempts to remove from us in our hearts. It is all up to you. It is your choice. You can take hold of your feelings and emotions and move forward with memories and thoughts of beauty and love. Your willingness to move through your thoughts will allow you to become aware of your emotions. The Messaging Process in this book will invite spirit to guide and purify your soul as you face the grief in your life. This is the way of healing, and you must believe from the depths of your being that you are on your way.

Many people use the creative process as a healing tool. Through divine guidance, I was allowed to create a collection of messages called Heavenly Messages ~ Forever In My Heart®. Each message was created to reach out to all who have experienced grief and to honor spirit. I know that writing each message and creating this Messaging Process brought healing to my heart. I believe they have the power to do the same for you. It is my greatest hope that these messages and the Messaging Process serve with comfort and love for all who have experienced loss. I hope this book allows you to discover a sense of peace and healing from within your scared being that will bless you and all others who may cross your path on this healing journey.

With Love, Light, and Peace,
Debra Ann

I dedicate this book to the memory of my beloved parents and to all who are no longer with us but whose spirits remain in our hearts forever.

Your vital energy is returning to the Source,

like the flowing stream returns to ocean.

Heaven is our Father. Earth is our Mother.

All people are our brothers and sisters, and all things are our companions.

In this gentle, peaceful journey.

You are forming one body with heaven and earth.

Entrust yourself in this transforming and nourishing care of the Cosmos.

Listen to the voice of Love in silence.

You have heard the Way.

Return home in Peace.

From a Confucian wisdom keeper and the book *Graceful Passages*

And for my beautiful children, Christopher and Deanna—with all my love—*forever.*

Contents

Chapter 1

What Is Spiritual Healing?

Healing may not be so much about getting better, as about letting go of everything that isn't you—all of the expectations, all of the beliefs—and becoming who you are.

— Rachel Naomi Remen

What is Spiritual Healing?

Healing is ever present. It is here with you now as you read this book. Healing is a gift so powerful that it moves our life and gives us breath at every moment. Since grief is one of the most challenging life experiences anyone can encounter it is vital to gain an understanding of a healing from a spiritual perspective. The process of healing often leads many people on a spiritual journey. During this journey, there are many discoveries and awakenings. The most profound and meaningful experiences often occur when there is a connection or reconnection to Higher Consciousness, Universal Source, Eternal Spirit, Higher Self, or the one word that expresses all these terms: God. It is God reminding you to remember your truth and return to your spirit. It is God calling you back home for this moment in time. Healing is God's message through pain as the way to discover the limitless power of spirit and love. There is a threefold experience in the path toward spiritual healing. It includes faith to believe in your healing, hope to know the truth, and love to be eternal. Be confident to know that you are healing and you are deserving of this gift.

Release from Your Sensory Self

> "For we have heard of your faith in Christ Jesus the leaning of your entire human personality on Him in absolute trust and confidence in His power, wisdom, and goodness and of the love which you [have and show] for all the saints God's consecrated ones"- Colossians 1:4AMP

The spiritual path toward healing from grief involves a release from your sensory self, which is the part of you that responds to the five senses and separates you from your spiritual nature. Sensory self is the aspect of your human nature that allows you to perceive and relate to your physical surroundings. The loss of someone you love challenges your sensory abilities because your reality has shifted. The way you perceive and relate to yourself, to others, and to your physical environment has changed. It is this shift in the nature of things that causes a change in your behavior and leads you to the experience of grief.

Grief draws you inward. It deafens the physical world as you make your way to the internal dwellings of your heart. At first there is intense silence so profound it that it hurts. Then, the silence leads to stillness, and there is a presence of spirit. In this gradual, almost motionless movement of grief, healing is present. As healing guides you through the darkness of loss and grief, you are moving toward the light of peace. Each step is a step toward the inner dwelling of your soul. The journey releases you from your sensory self as you discover the divine inner presence of spirit, your ultimate reality of Self with God.

You can think of the word *Grief* as *G*etting *R*eal *I*ntense *E*nergy *F*orever. If you think of grief in this way, you can see it as a healing journey of eternal spirit and energy that is with you every day. It is not here to hurt you; it is here to remind you of who you are and the truth of all spiritual existence. It may seem like a curse now, but eventually this energy will feel like a blessing because it will keep you connected to the spirit of your loved ones if you allow it to heal you as you move forward.

For years people who were grieving were told to move on, to get over it, or to accept the loss. Does anyone ever really do any of these things? Spirit cannot separate itself from itself. We were not meant to move away from love when death occurs. The sensation of love that burns in our hearts for our departed loved ones is there to let us know that love continues to flow and connect us to spirit even after death. It is the same love that allows you to continue to love when you thought you could never love again. The reason for this is that you are loving the One Spirit that exists in all of us because the One Spirit that exists in all us is loving you back through eternity.

This spirit is always expanding and giving. It travels beyond the physical limitations of the human sensory self, which perceives the circumstances of death as an ending or separation. As spirit makes its way, it is constantly moving with love. The way to healing is to surrender the physical limitations of the body and submit to the eternal existence of spirit. In this way you release all the preconceived suggestions about healing and allow for spirit to move through you and push you forward with supernatural strength by connecting you to infinite energy—to God. This connection to God is the only true source of healing that lives in you. God's healing power in you can lead you to the love that can overcome all things, even death.

Healing from grief is a gift given to all who have loved so much, and love is the eternal energy that fills the empty ache from which we grieve. So, no matter what you are told about where you should be at any given point during grief or no matter where you think you should be in the healing process, always know that you are where you are supposed to be. There is no set amount of time given for healing from grief, but if you are wondering if your pain will subside, then your questioning is a signpost that healing is at work in you. As long as you question, you are making yourself aware. It is your awareness toward healing that heals. Here lies your acceptance and movement through grief.

As you accept the moment, you can surrender and release the experience to God, who in turn offers you healing love and grace. You then have a choice: to receive the healing or to continue with the suffering and numbness of grief. Your free will can give you freedom if you allow God to move in you. The motion of God will help you to choose to create rather than react. Your life is shaped not by your experiences but by your reactions to them. You can choose to react by creating, and in this way you are behaving in the way God designed you to react. You can choose to create peace, love, and harmony by carefully becoming aware of your thoughts and your reactions to them. If you can react to a negative thought as a stimulus to create a positive thought, then you are reacting creatively.

As you are healing, keep in mind that there is no perfect way to heal. You can set yourself up for disappointment and frustration if you attempt to heal perfectly. Trying to do or have all things perfect brings frustration in all areas of life because you feel you cannot live up to your perfection. In order to heal, you need to forget yourself and find the state of beingness within you that is one with and trusts God as truly perfect. Trusting God will allow for the grace of God to be present through healing. You have the power of God or the universe waiting to open itself up and heal you. The Great Physician is within you. You really don't need to know more than this as you move on your spiritual path toward healing from grief.

Spiritual healing requires that you suspend your intellect and your will and submit to God. Whatever you have been told by others or by yourself, whatever you may think should have been or should be, and whatever your personal beliefs, desires, or knowledge may be, it all needs to be let go of and given to God. All of these aspects of the personal, sensory being are the human qualities within us that weigh down the ability to function at a higher level of thought. Once you have allowed yourself to experience the release from your sensory self, you become aware of the higher states of consciousness that promote spiritual healing.

John 19:17 tells of the place where Jesus was crucified, buried, and resurrected: "They took Jesus, therefore, and he went out bearing His own cross to a place called the Place of a Skull, which in Hebrew is called Golgotha." Golgotha is a place on a hill northwest of Jerusalem. Jesus demonstrated that in order to walk through the death experience you must enter a different place, outside the mind, a place of higher elevation. Jesus carried His cross into Golgotha where He suffered a great physical pain, died, and was resurrected to a new life. He rose above the suffering by releasing His human lower level of conscious thoughts (the Skull); with thoughts of higher consciousness (a rising on a greater hill).

You have the power to rise above the battle in your mind when you seek to enter the higher elevations of selfhood. Death is too complicated for the human sensory ability to grasp. The human mind cannot wrap itself around the concept of death.

The biblical scripture teaches that you have to enter a higher state of mind and elevate your consciousness to place of greater knowing outside the scope of human capabilities. This means we need to crucify the human aspects of our being—the flesh or sensory self—for spirit to reign. This will allow you to lift your suffering to a higher source in order to gain renewal and restoration. Also, this passage teaches that the cross is not only about suffering. The cross is a reference to the paths we all travel. The various paths of the cross include the healing path, the serving path, the giving path, and the loving path. Jesus walked through these paths for us as He carried the cross to teach and usher us through the spiritual healing journey. Your healing already exists in the spiritual realm. It is up to you to use your physical form and spiritual essence to follow the footprints that have already been traveled and discover the healing path.

God has said, "Every place that the sole of your foot shall tread upon, that have I given unto you." As you reflect on the cross, consider these thoughts: where are you traveling on your cross? Which path are you on? Also, it is interesting that the cross is the same symbol as the plus sign in arithmetic. This is because the cross is about positive transformation and resurrection to a new way of being. It is about adding to your life and to the life of others as you journey along its path. It may seem like you are carrying a heavy burden, but the cross is holding you up and supporting you with supernatural power and love. It is giving the power to travel a difficult path. This is a path that must be traveled to gain the infinite sum of all, the eternal love of God and eternal life. The path is your journey to your inner road of strength, peace, truth, wisdom, love and rest. It is the path to the presence of God within you that you travel toward through your life. Here is where you carry your cares and burdens so that you can have the security and assurance of God as your faithful guide toward healing. Allow the power of the cross to raise you to your new spiritual life through the love of Christ crucified. It has already been "given unto you."

The Gospel's account of the crucifixion tells us that Jesus was placed between two thieves when he was crucified on the cross. When one of them expressed faith in Jesus, Jesus answered, "Today shalt thou be in paradise." Jesus' suffering was beyond comprehension, but he was able to use whatever breath he had left to tell the thief about Salvation and with that breath Jesus spoke with awareness and presence. Within our own lives sometimes the suffering and pain are so unbearable that even the thought of taking the next breath seems impossible, but to follow the example of Jesus and allow awareness to be present can move you to your next breath with faith.

The location of the cross teaches that the center of all existence is held in the tender balance between life and death, which is the now or the moment. It allows us to be ever mindful of the present moment of the healing process. The position of Jesus' cross in the middle at Calvary allows for the balance of a centered spirit to merge the body and mind (the body and mind are represented by the two thieves positioned on the sides of Jesus). The cross offers balance to the trinity of your being by connecting your spirit with the body and mind so that you can endure the trials of life by merging with your divinity. Within all this triune existence, the middle demonstrates the mindful presence of the now, or God, in healing. The word triune defines the union of the body, mind with your divine spirit.

For instance, the placement of the words in the following phrases indicates the importance of a centered mind during healing: "the past, *present,* and future", or "the body, *mind***,** and spirit." The words, "present" and "mind" are in the center. Another instance of this is in a short hymn of praise to God called the "Glory Be," which is said in Roman Catholic and Anglican Churches.: "Glory be to the Father, and to the *Son*, and to the Holy Spirit. As it was in the beginning is *now* and ever shall be. World without end. Amen." Again, notice the placement of the words "Son" and "Now". This is an ever-present hymn and praise to God. The nature and mind of God, demonstrated in so many ways, is always centered on the present moment and the nowness of being. With healing it is vital to not look back or forward but to hold the mind centered on the presence of God through the moments.

To be present with the cross and the healing path in this way allows you to see the possibilities in the impossible. The cross offers purification and love to every person. Christ being crucified and raised on the cross allows our own suffering to be crucified and raised with him. Jesus pierced his sensory self to the cross. When you look at the cross, see your suffering and pain being nailed to the cross. Then do just as Jesus did and command your spirit to God so that you can ascend to new life. As you release your sensory self, you will allow yourself to tap into the divine inner senses and align yourself with God and spirit. It will allow you to surrender your personal will and enter the will of God. The chapter in this book on visualization, affirmation, and meditation offers spiritual practices with suggestions to guide you toward releasing your sensory self and discovering your inner spiritual nature.

The "Soul" Purpose for Healing

> "God whispers to us in our pleasures, speaks in our conscience, but shouts in our pains: it is His megaphone to rouse a deaf world.
>
> —C.S. Lewis

The sole purposes for healing are soul remembrance and soul awakening. Your soul wants to communicate with you and reveal to you your purpose and truth. The soul's purpose is to connect you to your heart and to the heart of all humanity. The trials in life allow God to contact you and give love to you so that Spirit can then love through you. It is God's grace moving through your graciousness. As the soul endeavors to reach this destination, you are merely a guest on the journey. You are discovering your eternal spirit, which is God's spirit in you. You are also discovering the spirits of all those you have loved and who have ever loved you, this is your inner life, your heaven. These discoveries through the healing journey allow you to be an inspiration for others who need to find the healing gift you have been given. In this way your healing is not just about you, but it includes the healing of every hurting heart that needs to discover truth and love.

Healing is given to one for the well-being of all as a gift that is shared by the collective soul. Here is where we find that we are not the separate, isolated beings that grief led us to believe about ourselves. Healing removes the dark veil that has covered our eyes and allows us to clearly see the luminous hand of God moving within and beyond ourselves. It is this light of God that touches and transforms every life with healing. Your pain, depression, grief, loss, or whatever hurts you, are all vibrating through the universe. However, it is your healing that holds a higher vibration, and it is this frequency that connects you to other souls in order to elevate the collective consciousness of the universe. Yes, your healing has that much power.

In your place—your tiny spot in the universe—you can choose to heal and to reach out with your healing to someone else. Then, a chain of healing can begin because you chose to create and behave in the way God designed you. The soul of every being has a direct relationship with the oversoul of the universe. Therefore, becoming free from your sensory self is God's design and purpose for your life. Freedom from your sensory self profoundly connects you to the divine love of God.

"All things work for good for those who love God and are called according to His design and purpose," Romans 8:28 is wisdom from the Bible that gives hope and meaning to whatever circumstances have hurt you in life. It allows you to believe that all the pain and suffering could be turned around and used for a higher good. This scripture allows us to understand that it is not because the experience is so bad that God can make it good, but rather that pure love is the divine essence of spirit and when this energy is brought to any experience it aligns everything to work together for the highest good of all. And it can—as you release yourself from your sensory being you are awakened and you remember your truth, the power of God, and your worth in this universe. You are the healing force God intended for you to be.

The Science of Healing

> "We have within us a power that is greater than anything that we shall ever contact in the outer, a power that can overcome every obstacle in our life and set us safe, satisfied and at peace, healed and prosperous, in a new light, and in a new life."
>
> -Ernest Holmes

The science of healing supports that there is a spiritual aspect to the healing process. God designed you with all the proper equipment you need to heal. Recent neurobiological theories have discovered that emotions are related to activities in the brain areas that focus our attention, motivate our behavior, and determine the importance of what is happening around us. The neurobiological explanation is based on discoveries made through the neural mapping of the limbic system within the brain. The limbic system is the area of the brain that supports our emotions, determines our behavior, and allows us to have long-term memory. An emotion is defined as a mental and physiological state associated with a variety of feelings, thoughts, and behaviors.

Your thoughts and feelings trigger emotional responses in the brain that allow you to react with a behavior. You have the ability to rewire the mapping of your brain by changing your thoughts and your reactions with positive emotions and behaviors. The science of healing provides you with the ability to reprogram the neurotransmitters in the brain in such a way that suggest that a healthy healing pattern can be realized within a thirty to forty day period of changing behavior. You are transmuting old patterns into healthy patterns. This is the alchemy of healing in the temple of the body. You are created to discover a healthy mental, physical, and spiritual path toward healing. This means there is a change from an imperfect, diseased state of being towards a perfect, healthy, and everlasting state. It is a change from mortal consciousness to the God consciousness of radiant light and love.

So, you are actually hardwired to heal yourself. Also, the link between science and spirituality (or body and spirit, created and creator, or finite and infinite) has lead to the discovery of amazing evidence that indicates that there is a connection between the heart and the brain. Recently, neuroscientists have discovered that the heart has its own independent nervous system called the "brain in the heart." Scientists have learned that there are over forty-thousand nerve cells in the heart and that it has an energy field five-thousand times greater than the brain. With this finding one can conclude that the feelings sent from the heart can have an enormous effect on brain functions to engage increased well-being and spiritual healing. This may be the reason why spirituality refers to the heart center as "the seat of the soul." To place all of your emotions, feelings, and thoughts within your spiritual center of the heart will allow you to sit them with the divine within you. Once this part of you has been released to your heart center, which is where the God of light resides, you will enter a peace that transcends all understanding and your mind will become engaged in higher thought patterns. Then, you will be able to stand up and face the battles of life so that you can begin healing.

From the perspective of dealing with grief, the sentiment of a broken heart is very real and intensely felt when a loved one passes. The brain and heart disconnect during grief because the death has caused the link that supports the transmission of love and other higher thought emotions to the brain to turn away from each other. However, the overflowing neurons within the heart can restore and regenerate the emotional connection that has been broken by grief and allow the brain to receive signals of powerful spiritual energy that can promote healing. To allow the intense energy of the heart to permeate your mind and soul with thoughts of love and spirit will provide healing during grief. The "brain in the heart" divinely knows how to merge the triune being toward wellness by becoming whole again.

Finally, a healing process that includes creativity is the most profound way to promote healing because you are attuned with the nature of God and all biorhythms are flowing in their natural balance of harmony. The body, mind, and spirit connection is an absolute essential on the healing journey.

Through the process of healing there is an awakening of consciousness. As your spirit becomes empowered it allows for your mind to enter a calm state of being that renews the body. Healing allows your triune being to become harmonized and balanced so you can elevate the energy fields within and around you. When you allow healing to be present, the gift to cultivate and support an inspired life unfolds and reveals to you truth. Your authentic self has emerged and you are free to heal and be a healing force through the challenges of life.

Chapter 2

What Is Grief?

Being deeply loved by someone gives you strength, while loving someone deeply gives you courage.

—Lao Tzu

Grief is itself a medicine. —William Cowper

What is Grief?

Grief can be explained as the response to the experience of death or loss. It varies from person to person. Although many try to clump the grief experience into a general pile of symptoms and stages, grief is a very personal and often isolating experience. Therefore, it is necessary to have a very clear and meaningful understanding of the grief process in order to move through it with presence and awareness.

Life brings many different experiences as we journey. Grief is an experience that can develop through various life circumstances. For example, the grief process may occur from life situations as a natural response to loss, these situations may include:

- A divorce or a separation of any kind of relationship
- Loss of health through a physical or emotional illness
- Loss of a personal dream by it either being unfulfilled or ended
- A serious illness of a loved one or friend
- Loss of a job or business
- Loss of financial stability
- Death of a pet
- The most intense grief—the death of a loved one.

For the purpose of this book we will focus on the passing of a loved one and how to move through the grief experience from a spiritual perspective. However, you can apply the process and spiritual practices in this book toward any grief experience you may be facing in your life. This chapter on grief is only a brief overview of the common stages related to the grief experience. It is provided only to impart a basic understanding of the phases of grief after loss.

In 1969, psychiatrist Elisabeth Kubler-Ross introduced the Five Stages of Grief as they are known today. They were first identified and based upon her studies of patients dealing with terminal illness, but now her studies are applied to other grief experiences, especially the loss of a loved one. Generally, there are five common stages of grief:

- Shock and Denial
- Pain and Guilt
- Anger and Bargaining
- Reflection and Loneliness
- Acceptance and Hope.

These stages are best described as emotional responses to the conditions of life after loss. Therefore, it is important to remember that not every stage or emotion will take place in the order given. In fact, you may not experience every stage of the grief process, or it may show up later on. Actually, almost anything you are feeling at the beginning of the grief process can be considered normal since you are attempting to integrate the intense and undefined experience of loss into your life. You may feel like you are living a nightmare, losing your mind, or questioning your spiritual beliefs. If you are feeling like this or you are having other emotions, please try not to judge, label or condemn these feelings. Try to allow yourself to be present with your thoughts and then let go of them or release them. Be kind and gentle to yourself. Grief is a natural process, and as it flows through you, it is allowing for your body, mind, and spirit to reconnect to life again.

Man, when he does not grieve, hardly exists. —Antonio Porchia

Let's take a closer look at the five stages of grief. In the stage of Shock and Denial you are first confronted with the experience of the loss of your loved one. Your initial response is disbelief, because you can't imagine what is actually happening, so your mind immediately knows to cushion the blow by offering you emotional protection for the pain. Your mind is literally denying the loss at some level, and the overwhelming internal voice that shouts "how could this be" or "this can't be happening" becomes soberly silenced by the numbing effects of shock and denial. For some, the loss can be so difficult to experience that they begin to deny the loss has actually happened. They may expect their loved one to appear even though they know they are gone. This can be normal and possibly needed for you until you can learn to be with the loss in some way. However, if denial becomes your coping mechanism then you will not be able to fully move through the experience of grief and you will be stuck in this painful existence.

We must embrace pain and burn it as fuel for our journey.
—Kenji Miyazawa

The Pain and Guilt phase of grief is the time when shock and denial have been transformed toward the reality of what has been lost. There is much suffering during this stage, because the awareness of separation is fully activated in the mind. The language during this stage may be, "I feel so sick with pain, I can't live" and "Maybe I could have done more or done something different." At times the pain may be unbearable, and you may want to escape it. Don't! You have to experience these emotions in order to heal. Please try not to use drugs or any alcoholic substance to minimize the pain. This may lead to a serious addiction. The pain is there because it should be. Your body, mind, and spirit are grieving the loss of someone you loved as well as the loss of part of yourself—the "you" that you came to know through them. So much has changed that your reality has shifted. However, the pain will assist you in realigning your life again. You must trust the pain, not fear it. There is so much pain in the change that the death experience brings to life. It is unbearably uncomfortable but the hope is that it is birthing a new life in you.

The guilt of this stage is also very intense. The emotion of guilt is often very strong and painful because your mind is trying to find reasons and explanations for this death. This is what the mind does when it feels it has lost control of a situation. Let your mind move through the guilt and know in your heart that love is greater than the condemnation of the mind. You will return to love once you allow yourself to feel the pain, and you will know that there is no blame, shame, or guilt associated with death. You can never hurt, blame, or shame yourself or anyone else to bring anyone back to life. Guilt deadens you to your reality. It is the temporary way your mind is trying to block the pain by refocusing on other unconstructive, negative thoughts. Pain and guilt are more accessible emotions than loss and grief, and your mind will easily choose to replace the harsh reality of loss with these lower thought patterns.

If you're going through hell, keep going. —Winston Churchill

In the Anger and Bargaining stage of grief you are so badly hurt and depressed that anger becomes the emotion that covers up what you are really feeling. The voice of this stage sounds like this, "This life has no meaning, or I am so mad at this person because they weren't there with me" and "If I give away 'this' or stop doing 'that' they will come back." The anger can be at yourself, someone else, or maybe at your loved one who passed. It is easier to feel anger than hurt. Anger can be more intense if the death of a loved one was caused by an event or another person. You can become so absorbed in anger that it can lead you to thoughts of revenge or making someone pay for your loss and pain. These thoughts are only your mind's way of rationalizing your loss.

The Bible passage in Psalm 139 says "the days allotted to me have all been recorded in your book before any of them ever began." Eventually you will come to realize that no one knows the time, place, or circumstance of how anyone will leave this earthly plane. Also, all deaths, even the most accidental or untimely as well as the most natural, occur as the way for each soul to move on. The how, when, or where of a death holds no value for the soul which has passed. They only knew that the time had come for them to make a transition to spirit. The circumstances or events of death are left behind for your own journey—for whatever lessons you are to learn from the death experience of your loved one. I know it is hard to think like this, but in the intricate web of life and death a balance exists that can either protect and assist you through grief or trap you and hold you back. It is how you choose to create and move through your pain that will decide your path.

Anger is the ugly mask of grief that you wear when you don't know who you are anymore. It is the disguise that allows you to walk through your pain as a stranger in your own world. It will be with you until you are ready to face what is underneath the mask and remove it so that you can live your life again.

Bargaining is another phase in grief that the mind uses to rationalize the death experience. If you inherited money or other assets, you may bargain with these as a way to bring back your loved one. You may feel that if they had known how unimportant all these other material things are to you, then they will return. You might even bargain with addictive behaviors by saying "if I stop or start doing this or that it will bring them back." This is another way of attempting to escape your reality and keep yourself stuck in the negative patterns of living.

> You can clutch the past so tightly to your chest that it leaves your arms too full to embrace the present. —Jan Glidewell

Reflection and Loneliness is a difficult stage of grief because it is at this time when you may find yourself needing personal time alone to reflect on your memories, the life that was, and also on the life that is now. The language during this stage may be, "I don't want to be with anyone right now; no one understands how I feel". You realize the significance of your loss during this stage. You may feel intense emptiness, loneliness, and despair. This is all normal as you create a space for the reality that is now in your life. In this place, you find yourself asking the higher questions; your soul is reaching for spirit's guidance, and you realize that you're broken.

During this stage, you can begin to release it all. Your emotional system is driving you home and you are becoming whole again. The veil of deception is being lifted and left behind in the shattered pieces of grief. A new masterpiece is being created. A beautiful mosaic of light is now forming in you. It is important that as you experience this phase of grief to remember that there is hope and light within and ahead of you. You have a future. Your future lies in your ability and strength to embrace and engage in life as it is right now. Your future can be defined as "nows" waiting your arrival. Each moment holds your future and your past. As I write this, the past has already been, and as I make my way to the next sentence, the future is waiting to happen. It is this momentary. Your healing through grief is the same. So, as you reflect and feel the silence and stillness of death, know that it is passing through you and guiding you to the next moment.

Moving moment by moment will allow you to embrace the present and your life again. Also, your loneliness may have been driven by well-intentioned family and friends who may have told you that they are concerned for you and feel you need to move on at this point. No one can tell you how to feel or act during grief: not this book or any other book—no one! So, even the most heartfelt person can seem unwelcomed and meaningless to you. The loneliness is necessary for you as you welcome a time for reflection at this stage. Every aspect of the stages in grief allow your emotions to guide, protect, and heal you. Spirit or God will use all things for your good, even the pain and sorrow from this experience. The power within you propels forward every moment with love, hope, and peace. As you reflect, you will feel the comforting embrace of spirit, and you will know that you are not alone. The book of Job says, "I am secure and feel confident because there is hope, yes; I look around and take my rest in safety. I lie down and none make me afraid.". Allow yourself to take a moment to rest and reflect. Know you are not alone, but "all one" with God.

> There are things that we don't want to happen but have to accept, things we don't want to know but have to learn, and people we can't live without but have to let go. —Author Unknown

Reflection and Loneliness will move you toward the stage of Acceptance and Hope. The word "acceptance" may seem inappropriate in this stage because no one can say that they accept the passing of their loved one. Accepting for some would imply that one might be approving of the death of their loved one. To associate these meanings with the word "acceptance" in grief may make it difficult to promote healing. A better way to understand the word "acceptance" in this stage is to exchange it with words like "love" or "embrace." These new words allow you to see that it is not the death of your loved one that should be accepted, loved, or embraced but the reality that death has brought to your life. That is to say, it's not good that your loved one died, you don't approve of it, you didn't want, you don't like it, and it's unacceptable and thoughts like these should be released or surrendered to God. But it happened. It is the reality of your life now. So, it is the reality of what is happening in your life right now that you have to move toward with thoughts of acceptance and love. This reality cannot be changed.

When you can't accept life's changes, you are fighting with reality. You are resisting life. When you fight with reality, it is a losing battle, and no one wins. The change that death has brought to your life is real and will be a part of you forever. It has changed your being and the way you live. Allow yourself to look at your life with new eyes and see it for what it is. There is hope for a new way of being, living, and moving through life. Although it is difficult, you now must create a different dream to dream. There are adjusted visions to fulfill in your life. You can begin to say, "I can love from this place again. I am whole. I am never alone because spirit is always by my side. I am strong, and I allow myself to be alive again."

If you wipe away the despair and allow love and spirit to shine through, you will learn not only to accept this experience but you will embrace it with all your heart as you let it heal you from the inside out. And it is in this place of the heart, where the presence of God abides. This is your sacred home of love and spirit. The place where you discover your hope for eternity. Acceptance of your reality with thoughts of love will move you toward *Hope,* which is *H*aving *O*nly *P*eace *E*veryday or *H*aving *O*nly *P*ositive *E*nergy.

You cannot be hopeless when you have positive energy in your life. You cannot be hopeless when you have peace in your soul every day. When you have positive energy, there is love. Where there is love, there is peace. When there is love and peace, there is hope. And where there is hope, there is God. You can have only peace everyday when you live your life with the treasures of love and spirit that are in your heart. This gift of peace offers you security and unity through grief as you heal. In the words of Thomas Campbell, "To live in the hearts we leave behind is not to die."

The pain passes, but the beauty remains. —Pierre Auguste Renoir

Often, many who experience grief ask the question, "What happens if grief doesn't go away?" The truth is that you will always miss your loved one who has passed. The desire to have them with you each and every day of your life will remain. It doesn't matter how many years have passed since the day you lost someone you love, you will still think of them and miss them. Because you loved them so much, their beauty remains in your heart. This is the normal way of life after loss for many of us who have grieved. However, when grief is out of balance, the pain and loss becomes so overwhelming that you feel you no longer want to engage in life. The grief has complicated your ability to live life. You may find that the loss has impacted your ability to relate to others or you may be having difficulty moving through normal, everyday routines. In the beginning of grief, this can be normal but as you move on through grief the way of life will seem to flow to you again so that you can move forward to be and do once more. You will need to become aware of your behaviors and feelings because they will allow you to know if the grief is moving forward without complications. However, if your grief is causing complications or emotional difficulty such as depression, then your ability to become aware of your behaviors and feelings will be challenging.

Although grief is a personal experience, there are times when a person should seek out professional assistance in order to move through the experience with support and guidance. When grief becomes overwhelming and you find yourself having difficulty engaging in life, please use every resource that is available to assist you. There are many qualified therapists who specialize in grief counseling as well as local grief support groups and local church or spiritual groups. Consider researching your area for any form of outreach that can provide you with care you need during this time. Your physician can also recommend the proper resources for you. Always remember that you are not alone. Help and support are out there. Please be diligent in finding the resources that can assist you during grief. With the help of professionals and spirit to guide you there is hope that "the pain will pass, but the beauty will remain."

Chapter 3

A Spiritual Path toward Healing

Visualizations, Affirmations, Prayer, and Meditation

The personal life deeply lived always expands into truths beyond itself.

—Anäis Nin

The Spiritual Path toward Healing

The spiritual path toward healing utilizes the techniques or practices of visualization, affirmation, prayer, and meditation. It is during these practices that one travels the inner road to the true life within their being. While there, you will discover your divine union with spirit and allow pure love to fill your heart, purify your soul, and drench your spirit with its truth and beauty. These practices will allow you to fortify a spiritual foundation. I only offer these to you for your consideration because they were useful to me in my own healing journey. If you should read something that resonates with you, consider applying it to your healing journey as well. Let's begin to explore these practices and techniques that are a part of spiritual path toward healing.

Visualization

> So we fix our eyes not on what is seen but what is unseen. For what is seen is temporary, but what is unseen is eternal.
>
> —2 Corinthians 4:18

Visualizations are a vital part of the healing process. For some, it may be difficult to engage in this process during grief. I remember being unable to close my eyes to sleep, never mind visualizing. Throughout my life, especially as a young girl, I had always felt the comfort of closing my eyes and going within. I didn't know then I was reaching into my divinity. I only knew it brought me to a better place and gave me peace.

Several years later, I had to deal with a traumatic death that made closing my eyes unbearable. Without the ability to sleep and relax, life became very challenging. However, I continued to resist closing my eyes because all I saw were tormenting memories. Through resistance the suffering persisted. Grief had covered my heart and buried my soul. I couldn't see inside myself any longer, which meant my spirit had been blinded. I had lost my peace. I felt disconnected from myself and my life. The suffering was not only emotional, but it had become physical as well. There were many ways in which my physical life had diminished but I will only tell you about the one that pertains most to visualizing.

After years of living with insomnia and depression, I had become unhealthy. One of the manifestations of illness in my body was when I developed a growth in the cornea of my left eye. The growth had been there for a while but had never been anything to be alarmed about until I noticed changes in its size and shape. I went to my ophthalmologist who felt the growth was suspicious and he sent me to ophthalmology oncology specialists for an evaluation. I was told that surgery was needed to remove the growth and then a biopsy would determine if it were malignant. I was horrified, not only about the potential of losing my eye, but also because I knew that I would be required to keep my eyes closed for a significant amount of time during and after the procedure. The surgery left a huge, gashed hole in my cornea; however, the growth was benign. The process of healing meant I had to keep a bandage over the left eye while the cornea mended. The stitches in my eye did not dissolve properly and I felt like fork prongs were stuck in my eye, and closing both eyes gave me some relief. I remained with my eyes closed for more than a week. During that time, I allowed myself to visit the memories that tormented me so much. I had no choice but to be with them and let them unfold in my mind's eye.

The experience was the most healing time since the passing of my loved ones. I saw the beauty in the ugliness of death. I was able to see above the physical with divine vision from within. I was grateful for an experience that forced me to close my eyes and discover truth. I know there are worse things than this, but I share this with you because I don't ever want you to get to the point where you are threatened with an eye malignancy and have to experience a huge gouge and prongs in your cornea to bring you to your divine vision.

When spirit wants to reach you, the boundaries are limitless, and it may use the body and mind to make contact. Without resistance, you allow for a balance within your triune being and there is harmony.

Visualizations provide the ability to see yourself and your situation as healed and whole. This will assist you to integrate the body, mind, and spirit throughout your healing. Through visualizations, the spiritual and physical aspects of your being become one. It allows you to see life and its experiences the way God sees it. You will discover the perfect in the imperfect. This is where true beauty exists in life. You are peeking through God's eyes when you visualize.

There are many reasons why people use visualizations. Some may find themselves in a financial crisis, and they can visualize themselves as prosperous and successful, doing the work they love. Some may be ill, and they can visualize themselves healthy, free from disease, living their life with well-being. Visualizing yourself in this way is beneficial because prosperous and healthy are your true states of being. You are seeing yourself "as if" it were already true, which is a very powerful vision because this is your truth in the mind of God.

For those who grieve, visualizations require deeper awareness because there is a struggle between the physical and spiritual entities. The struggle is that we are creatures of physical sensory behavior, therefore, when a loved one passes, there is a disconnect as a result of the inability to utilize the sensory ability. You can no longer see, hear, or touch your loved one, and so your reality has shifted from the seen to the unseen. Visualizing, especially during grief, requires you to focus your inner sight on the light of God within you. To visualize the light within and all around you connects you to the eternal spirit of love and truth. The light of God will dispel the darkness through grief and lead you toward an inner knowledge of divine unity.

Most of us have an understanding that we are spiritual beings living a human existence. I would like to share some thoughts about this topic because it can be especially difficult to close your eyes to visualize when hurtful thoughts are disrupting the peace and unity that exists within you. This concept of spiritual beingness can become diminished on the mind of a grieving person, because the feeling of separation is so intense. The feeling of separation disconnects the mind from the heart and opens the door to doubt, shame, regret, and other painful emotions. For instance, a person may be very sorrowful because they were not able to say goodbye or other sentiments were left unspoken. Another might be that a person may not have been with their loved one when they passed and there is sadness that they died alone, or a person was with their loved one when they passed and they wished they could have done more for them in some way. Yet another circumstance may involve the kind of death, possibly an accident or some other trauma that is causing intense grief.

Quantum physics explains that at the base of all creation there is a unified field of energy or consciousness that supports the entire universe. In a universe with divine order such as this, can there really be such a thing as an accident or coincidence? It may help to understand that what can be perceived as accidental is really a precise moment in time that could not have been avoided. Or if this is too painful to understand right now, then try to permit an understanding that divine order is making a way through the unthinkable and tragic as it heals your heart.,

The Centers for Disease Control reports that, aside from accidents and homicide, suicide is the third leading cause of death in people between the ages of fifteen and twenty four and the fourth leading cause of death in children between the ages of ten and fourteen. Although these facts pertain to the young population, mental illness and depression are diseases that many people battle regardless of age. A disease of the mind can be just as deadly as a disease of the body, such as cancer. Although the diagnosis and symptoms are usually less obvious for depression as opposed to a terminal cancer, the prognosis is the same. A disease is a "dis-ease" regardless of the way it manifest itself.

Every thought, every action, every decision, and every aspect of free will creates divine appointments, in whatever form they may be in, within every life. So we must know that with every gift of life a gift of free will is given. We must also know that the life span of any person is not one moment more or less that it was suppose to be. Some might even say that, at the spiritual essence of every soul, there is an inner knowing of the exact moment of how and when it will exit this earth plane. This moment is not known to the conscious level of the mortal mind. However, every death, whether it be natural or not, unfolds just as it is supposed to according to each soul's spiritual inner knowing When a person's soul's purpose in this world is concluded, no matter their age in years, their time here is complete. When Jesus died on the cross, his last words were, "It is finished". This meant he had completed the purpose and mission of his soul. The same is true for every person in regard to their souls' purpose and fulfillment. When it is the time to transit to eternal spirit the soul knows, and the events will unfold according to that subconscious knowing.

All this may seem like a lot to comprehend and that I am very matter of fact about these circumstances, but please know that I feel for you in whatever your pain might be and my hope is for you to heal. I write this description of mortality only to release the heaviness from your heart. There may be circumstances that I did not mention that can be causing your grief. In whatever is hurting you, always know that the energetic connection of spirit is always whole and perfect. It cannot be separated or broken. Spirit is always with us; no one is ever alone when they die or at any other time in life. Our words and actions are never measured in spirit because spirit speaks through us and acts for us as needed. All death, in whatever form it takes, is a shift in form from the physical to a return to the spiritual. The spirit is eternal.

It helps to understand that healing from the loss of a loved one often leaves you feeling open and raw. During grief, you may find that many situations will trigger emotional reactions that you may have never felt before in your life. You may find yourself feeling that way as you read this book or in your daily life. This is very normal, because healing involves accepting the moments that bring peace and comfort to your heart as well as the moments that bring discomfort and tension. Both are with you to offer you healing and release.

Those of us who are left behind in loss can sometimes feel like a circuit box that has been left unattended during a storm. Like circuits, emotions can flare and be triggered at any time. The storm is there to let you know which circuits are too short to withstand the power of the storm. An intense storm can short a circuit in an instant. It can only be adjusted once the circuit has been re-aligned with its power source. If at any time you feel as if you're short circuited, your fuse is too short, or something is hitting a nerve, know that this is where the eye of the storm exists for you and its pouring down and bringing these emotional outages to allow you to heal. Since this is not only a book about spiritual healing but also about emotional healing, you will be given the opportunity to explore and learn from every emotion that surfaces during grief. You will learn to understand yourself through the pain of the emotional outbursts that often strike like a bolt of lightning. You will experience healing as you align your emotions with the power of truth.

Now, let's get back to visualizations. Below is a visualization that will help you to gain an awareness of the perfection within the oneness of spirit. This will provide you with a metaphysical approach to meet the above circumstances of loss. Once you have worked with this visualization you will eventually be able to use your own inner guidance to journey into your divine vision through God. I hope the following visualization can be applied to ease your sorrow and offer you peace and healing in some way.

Let's begin the visualization:

Before you visualize, consider going to a comfortable place such as a favorite room, chair, or bed. You can sit with your feet up or lay down in a reclined position. Since your breathing is connected to the autonomic nervous system and mind, it should be calm and relaxed. The most preferable way to breathe is with your diaphragm. Place your hand slightly above your navel and breathe with your diaphragm by sending your inhalation down to that area. You will feel your abdomen expand. Hold the inhalation and count to eight. Then exhale through your mouth with a count to eight. Do this about three times and you should begin to feel the stress melting away from you. This breathing sequence will relax and pace your breathing. Once again, just be comfortable. Also, consider the smell, temperature, and lighting of the area. Please adjust each to your preferences. It may soothe your mind to light a fragranced candle that sends a pleasing scent into the atmosphere. Consider scents like lavender, vanilla, or chamomile.

After you have read the visualization below you will know the journey or you can have someone read the passage to you as you experience the visualization. Either way, once you are ready, just allow yourself to relax, close your eyes and remain still and quiet. Your inner guidance and divine vision will show you the way.

You are walking along the shoreline on a beach. The day is warm and bright with sunshine. As you walk you can feel the wet, soft sand under your feet. The gentle breeze feels soothing as it sweeps over your face. You stop for a moment to appreciate the beauty of the vast ocean in front of you. The sound of the ocean waves is melodic and flowing. The smell of the ocean is refreshing and revitalizing.

You notice the gulls pass you by as they sing their own song of praise for the day. As you turn to continue your walk, you see a blazing ray of light coming from the sun. This is God's light. As you move closer toward the light, you notice a familiar person moving toward you. It is your loved one, who is vibrant, healthy, strong, and happy. As you both move closer together, you tenderly reach for one another's hand. Then you pull each other in for a warm, loving embrace. This is a moment of pure joy.

The only words you say are, "I love you."

Your loved one slowly takes a step away and looks into your eyes and replies, "I love you too. I am always with you."

Here in this place there are no other words to say and nothing more to do except to fully immerse yourself in the loving union of this moment. You gently hold your loved one's face in your hands and smile. There is so much love and gratitude right now. As you both stay together in appreciation for each other and the moment, you sense the glowing light that brought forth your loved one as it embraces the two of you. The light is so bright, pure, and warm. You are being caressed by spirit. It is comforting, safe and peaceful.

You see yourself and your loved as whole and perfect. You are peaceful, calm, safe, and content. You are both surrounded by the glorious beauty of nature, eternal light, and spirit. Your loved one gently touches the heart center of your chest with their hand. You understand the meaning and gracefully acknowledge by placing your hand on top of your loved one's hand. You both close your eyes. There is an energy exchange of pure love. As you share this moment, you are both absorbed in light. The light of God is within and around both of you. You are still and at peace.

Before you awaken, you hold this image of your loved one within you, and you know that God will let this love, spirit, peace, and togetherness abide in you. There is love above you, love below you, love around you, and love within you. As you open your eyes, you feel the beauty and peace of this moment. You are now awake and one with spirit and eternal love as you carry your loved one in your heart.

This poem by ee cummings paints a beautiful picture of the heart and its connection to the eternal:

i carry your heart with me(i carry it in
my heart)i am never without it, anywhere
i go you go, my dear; and whatever is done
by only me is your doing, my darling,
i fear no fate(for you are my fate, my sweet) i want
no world(for beautiful you are my world, my true)
and it's you are whatever a moon has always meant
and whatever a sun will always sing is you

here is the deepest secret nobody knows

(here is the root of the root and the bud of the bud
and the sky of the sky of a tree called life; which grows
higher than the soul can hope or mind can hide)
and this is the wonder that's keeping the stars apart

i carry your heart(i carry it in my heart)

You can also use this guided meditation setting to visualize yourself meeting your angel or another divine being. Visualizations are beautiful and powerful ways for your body to visit the soul and spirit. Your soul is a mirror to your true life. When you spiritually look into your soul, you will discover and know yourself as whole and complete. You no longer feel the emotional and physical limitations of the body when you visualize through your soul in spirit. You are diving into the waves of spirit and letting the current sweep you away to the unknown place in the depths of your soul. As you journey to this divine inner sanctuary, you are a welcomed guest who is grateful and honored to visit with the sacred being of life within you.

Visualizing allows you to transcend the normal way we tend to see the circumstances in our lives. The more frequently you close your eyes and use your divine vision, the easier it will be to see the divine in your life when your eyes are open. The reason for this is because you are in direct contact with God, or your Higher Self, when you go within.

Many times during my own private moments I meditate on the Blessed Mother, Mary. You do not have to believe in Christianity to look and meditate on the life of Mother Mary. I wondered how she was able to watch her son be tortured, tormented, and crucified without ever attempting to save him. I thought to myself, how can a mother endure to see such intense brutality, suffering, and pain of her son? I dwelt in my heart with many thoughts. I asked, as she watched Jesus be tortured and put to death, did Mary reflect back in her mind to the days when he was her little baby? I would wonder if she could see herself carrying his little body, touching his little feet and hands, feeling his heart beat.

Did Mary think back to all the first moments in his life? There may have been thoughts of Jesus' first words, the first time he said "Mommy," first footsteps, holding his little hand to help him make his way, and how proud and marvelous those moments were for her. And as all this suffering and torture was happening to her son, did she remember him as he was growing up? She may have reflected back to their talks, times of laughter, or wiping away tears from his face—all the beautiful moments shared between a mother and child.

Then, finally, at the end of her son's life, when his brutally beaten, bloody body was removed from the cross and placed in her arms, what could have been Mary's thoughts? The sorrow and pain of this moment is too intense for my heart to even imagine. I could only think I could feel the brokenness in my heart and soul, but the truth is I can't bring myself to go there. It hurts too much. But that's me, the human aspect of my being. I know it was different for Mary. I have visualized Mary wiping the blood from her son's brow and holding him ever so close to her heart for a last embrace as she silently whispered with tethered breath, "It is finished." She knew her son had fulfilled the purpose of his soul. God's plan for salvation had been made complete. Death died and eternal life was born through the divine nature of a man and a woman.

These were my thoughts as I contemplated Mary. Maybe you may have had the same thoughts at some time as well. For some, Mary and Jesus can be just characters in the book of time. But if you really meditate and reflect on the lives of people such as this, it can offer you great strength and healing. For so many who are grieving, especially for those whose children have passed, Mary offers strength. She is a true example of a mother's grieving heart. Many who grieve through the loss of any of their loved ones have turned to her for consolation, because she can understand their sorrow. For this reason, I would continue to meditate and seek her grace. After careful listening to my heart, I realized, or "real eyes," that she did not submit to the human functions of mind. This would have separated her from God; it would have detached her from the divine and all that is true.

Could it be possible that she saw her son and all that was around her in their truest forms? This is not to say that she didn't see the suffering and deeply feel the pain of losing her son, but during The Passion where there was suffering, through Mary's eyes she saw strength. Where there was scorn, through Mary's eyes she saw the benevolence of her son. Where there was hate, through Mary's eyes she saw love—the eternal love of her son. Where there was fear, through Mary's eyes she saw faith. Where there was death, she saw life—eternal life and spirit. Yes, sorrow like a sword pierced her heart, but in despair she had hope in God.

The Blessed Mother helps us to understand that the physical world is a manifestation of the mind. You see what your mind manifests. If you look with the eyes of God, you will have mystical vision of divine love and truth. She helps us to understand how to let go of the attachments of the things on earth that separate us from heaven. Her way of being encourages us to always keep our consciousness in a state of higher thought toward Self and God. The symbolism of Satan under her feet can provide meaning for not walking in lower states of consciousness. These would be negative thoughts, actions, words or emotions. The crowning of stars around her head could represent the light of heaven surrounding her (or your) mind, which can allow light to manifest from above toward elevated states of awareness.

Through Mary, you come into relationship with her divine son, Jesus Christ, and the nature of God. The Blessed Mother gives the gift of perfect love through her Immaculate Heart. She has been called "The Seat of Wisdom" for the impartation of understanding and grace at times of difficulty. The heart of Mary holds every grieving heart with compassion, comfort, consolation, and healing. From a universal spiritual perspective, Mother Mary represents the divine feminine energy of the motherhood of God within every spirit and soul manifested through the qualities of creativity, intuition, grace, compassion, healing, and love.

In whatever you may understand or what you may believe about the Blessed Mother, one thing is true: there is much wisdom and grace to learn from her inspirational way of being and moving through life. Perhaps visualizing, peaking through God's eyes, can bring us a bit closer to our ability to see the divine within and all around us with pure eyes as Blessed Mother Mary. I pray for her to impart her divine strength and grace on every grieving heart. You can take your grief, sorrow, and pain from loss to the Mother Mary and to God the Father because Jesus Christ, the Son, was infinitely given for the suffering and love of all who grieve. To reflect and meditate on the gift of eternal life given to each of us through Christ can offer healing to all who mourn the passing of their loved ones.

Affirmations

> One comes to believe whatever one repeats to oneself sufficiently often, whether the statement be true or false. It comes to be the dominating thought in one's mind.
>
> —Robert Collier

Affirmations are necessary for the healing process because they allow you to speak spiritual truths into your physical existence. As we become more spiritual, we begin to remember our true Selves and God. As seekers of truth we must be speakers of truth too. Words are very powerful. They hold all of creation. You can become empowered by affirming powerful truths to your life and being. Have you ever heard someone say "they are going to eat those words"? Well, there is a very metaphysical truth to this saying. Our thoughts and actions are nourished by our words, which will form our life. Words carry weight and energy.

It is important to exercise self control, restraint, and right choice with the words you speak. It is a spiritual discipline. This will allow you to travel through life lightly. Words release energy as seeds for creation. What you say matters, literally. To use the power of the spoken word with respect and integrity toward yourself and others is a universal principle of spirit and reality. The Bible teaches in Proverbs 18:21, "The power of life and death are in the tongue, and they who indulge in it shall eat the fruit of it." You can choose to speak life, which is vital energy, over life's circumstances even when you are weakened by its trials. This will revitalize your being. Only you have the power to change your life. Living a positive, empowered, healthy life honors you and your loved one.

There are many ways to use affirmations. Some may practice affirmations for empowerment and overcoming negativity with an emphasis on religious beliefs, while others practice affirmations that are more universal and/or spiritual in nature. You should practice whichever you most believe in and the approach which is most comfortable for you. You could even mix it up a bit if you feel like there is an affirmation that speaks to your heart. Once you chose to implement affirmations into your life, you will notice positive changes in your being, presence, and the world around you. Affirmations offer healing to the grieving heart because the heart knows when it hears truth since truth is all the heart knows. It is our minds that deceive our hearts. Affirmations create a balance between the heart and mind through the application of truth, which is the affirmation itself; action, which is speaking it out of your mouth; and faith, which is to know you have the power to do this and to "know thyself." It aligns the spirit with the physical by impressing the subconscious mind with a transforming positive truth.

If you are uncomfortable speaking affirmations out loud to yourself, then make a list of affirmations and read from it silently. Either way is fine because you will be reinforcing the positive over the negative. Consider reading or saying them repeatedly throughout the day, especially when a negative feeling or thought begins to emerge. Please understand that in order for affirmations to be effective there must be a belief in the words you are affirming.

Obviously, you are not trying to ignore your feelings. If you have very recently lost a loved one, then it is important for you to allow your emotions and thoughts to be present. Whatever you push away will only come back at another time. This grief process is about acknowledging and honoring yourself and the memory of your loved one with love and gentleness. Please be patient with yourself. If you are not ready, then place all of this aside. You can come back to it at another time. There is a Buddhist proverb that says when the student is ready the teacher will appear. The teacher is nowhere but inside of you. The inner spirit teaches from within. So, only you will know when the time is right to practice any of these techniques. However, if you are in a place where you feel your inner guidance is ready to move through your emotions, then these processes will help.

My own experience has been that there are many ways to affirm spiritual principles into life, but the most profound transformations occur when one is in union with the word of God through Jesus Christ. Within my life, I have seen miraculous healings come forth from catastrophic illnesses such as cancer and emotional and addictive diseases. The benevolent wisdom of spirit has the power to heal you from any circumstance in life. I believe there is great power in the name of Jesus Christ and would encourage anyone to call upon His name whenever the need should arise in life. I often close my eyes and quietly and reverently repeat the name of Jesus whenever I need peace, calm, and help at any time in my life. The name of Jesus Christ affirms the healing power of God through the Christ consciousness within me. It also affirms the resurrection to new life and way of being.

In my life, especially when dealing with grief, there has been no greater healer than my relationship with Jesus Christ, and for this I am eternally grateful. I say this not as a religious statement from any church, doctrine, or dogma. I say this because I have had experiences of healing through faith and spirit throughout my life. Once these experiences have been given to the mind of any human, faith becomes unshakeable. The knowing of the sacred consciousness within our being allows for a discovery of truth and peace. This aligns the soul and spirit. You can consider affirming the name of Jesus as well, and see if your heart feels the power of consciousness within you by simply saying His name. Again, it is much more meaningful to affirm whichever practices are true to your heart. You may say another name of a divine being that resonates with you. It helps to remember that these are only names and words created through the human language. Although as humans we consider these names to be sacred, what really matters the most is that you connect to the existence of your sacred inner truth with whatever words or names you choose to affirm.

You can consider saying any of the following suggested statements to affirm over your life, or you can create your own affirmations. Your inner knowing will guide you toward the affirmations that offer you healing and peace. If any of the affirmations resonate with your heart, then your inner being has found the guidance it seeks. Spirit always finds its way to and through you. Allow the spiritual vibrations of the affirmations you choose to say to penetrate and be absorbed into the very essence of your being. As you say any of these affirmations, you will align your emotional vibrations with the frequency of the universe. Below are some scriptural, universal, and spiritual references that you can use as affirmations for healing if you are interested. Affirmations are always spoken in the present such as "I am" or "I have." Please slowly speak them aloud or to yourself with awareness and intention.

You can profess the word of God by affirming scriptures from the Bible. When saying the scriptures out loud or to yourself be sure to use "I," "my," or "me" wherever possible.

Below are some healing scriptures from the Bible: These scriptures allow for the powerful word of God to be spoken over your life.

> For the word of God is alive and powerful. It is sharper than the sharpest two-edged sword, cutting between soul and spirit, between joint and marrow. It exposes our innermost thoughts and desires.—Hebrews 4:12

If you are feeling lonely, isolated, or rejected, speak these scriptures as affirmations for your life:

The Lord is close to the brokenhearted and saves those who are crushed in spirit.—Psalms 34:18 NIV

You, O Lord, are a shield for me, my glory and the lifter of my head.—Psalms 3:3

I am overcome with joy because of God's unfailing love, for He has seen my troubles and He cares about the anguish of my soul.—Psalms 31:7 NLT

I know that your goodness and love will be with me all my life and your house will be my home as long as I live.—Psalms 123

I have set the Lord always before me. Because He is at my right hand I will not be moved.—Psalms 16:8

Jesus said, I'm telling you these things while I'm still living with you. The Friend, the Holy Spirit whom the Father will send at my request, will make everything plain to you. He will remind you of all the things I have told you. I'm leaving you well and whole. That's my parting gift to you. Peace. I don't leave you the way you're used to being left—feeling abandoned, bereft. So don't be upset. Don't be distraught.—John 14:27 The Message

God has good thoughts and plans toward me. He intends for me to have peace and not evil and to give me hope in my final outcome.—Jeremiah 29:11

I can do everything through him who gives me strength.—Philippians 4:13 NIV

If you are feeling fear, anxiety, or stress, speak these scriptures as affirmations for your life:

I sought the Lord and He heard me, He delivered me from all my fears.—Psalms 34:4

But He knows the way I take; when He has tested me, I will come forth as Gold.—Job 23:10 NIV

He will keep me safe from all hidden dangers and from all deadly diseases. He will cover me with His wings and I will be safe in His care.—Psalms91:3–4

Your eyes saw my unformed substance, and in Your book all the days [of my life] were written before ever they took shape, when as yet there was none of them.—Psalms 139:16

Thy word is a lamp unto my feet and a light unto my path. —Psalms 119

He gives me new strength and guides me on the right paths as He has promised.—Psalms 123

The Almighty is beyond our reach and exalted in power; in his justice and great righteousness, he does not oppress.—Job 37:23

Jesus said, I have told you these things, so that in Me you may have [perfect] peace and confidence. In the world you have tribulation and trials and distress and frustration; but be of good cheer [take courage; be confident, certain, undaunted]! For I have overcome the world. [I have deprived it of power to harm you and have conquered it for you.]—John 16:33

Jesus said, Peace I leave with you, My peace I now give and bequeath to you. Not as the world gives do I give to you. Do not let your hearts be troubled, neither let them be afraid. Stop allowing yourself to be agitated and disturbed; and do not permit yourselves to be fearful and intimidated and cowardly and unsettled.—John 14:27

God has not given me a spirit of fear and timidity, but power, love and self-discipline.—2 Timothy 1:7 NIV

If you are feeling guilt, shame, or depressed, speak these scriptures as affirmations for your life:

Arise, shine, for your (my) light has come and the glory of the Lord rises upon you (me).—Isaiah 60:1 NIV

New honors are constantly bestowed on me, and my strength is continually renewed.—Job 29:20 NLT

Weeping may last for a night, but a song of joy comes in the morning.—Psalms 30:5 GWT

Ask and you (I) will receive, and your (my) joy be complete.—John 16:24 NIV

The thief comes only to steal, kill and destroy. Jesus came so that I may have life and have it abundantly.—John 10:10

For God so loved the world that he gave His one and only Son, so that whoever believes in Him shall not perish but have eternal life.—John 3:16 NIV

I am assured and know that God works all things out for good because I love Him and I am called according to His design and purpose.—Romans 8:28

For as one thinks in his heart, so is he.—Proverbs 21:5 KJV

The Lord has declared that He will restore me and heal my wounds.—Jeremiah 30:17 NIV

I pray that I may enjoy good health and that all may go well with me, even as my soul is getting along well.—3 John: 2 NIV

Here are some universal and spiritual affirmations: universal affirmations allow for all truth from the consciousness of light and spirit to be spoken into your life.

If you are feeling lonely, isolated, or rejected, speak these affirmations for your life:

I am one with all, and all is one with me.

I now rest in a state of peace, and I am one with Eternal Spirit.

Nothing can stand before me when God stands with me.

I release all negativity toward myself and others. I am a harmonious being.

The love, wholeness, and completeness of God fill my heart every moment of every day.

I am eternal energy and spirit. I am one with the Creator.

I move with the wisdom of the divine and its infinite direction. As the universe or God moves, so I move.

I walk in the Light of the Kingdom of Heaven every day.

If you are feeling fear, anxiety, or stress, speak these affirmations for your life:

The Light of God has dissolved unwanted thought patterns from my mind.

I am joy. I am peace. I am calm. I am safe. I am love.

I am embracing life with passion.

I am confident and strong every day. With Universal Spirit my soul and its destiny are fulfilled, and I have a complete feeling of happiness throughout my being.

Through the courage and silence of my heart I make a decision to change. I love myself.

Since the Universe itself is behind me, all circumstances are favorable for me at this moment. The God within me is greater than any feeling of self doubt within me. I accept that all is made well already. I nullify all negative thoughts to the light.

The Light is always with me to shine on my way in life, and it aligns me with spirit.

If you are feeling guilt, shame, or depressed, speak these affirmations for your life:

The Power of God within me is great and mighty, and my mind is made new.

The healing Power of the Inner Light, God within me, is healing me now.

I am a child of God. I am a son or daughter of God and God is pleased with me.

The healing power of God is healing me from the crown of my head, throughout my body, to the soles of my feet.

Every negative experience serves as a signal to my mind to react positive and spiritual.

I release everything in my life that does not serve for God and my highest good, and all is immediately replaced with the healing light of God's love.

I attune my mind each day to the Infinite Presence of God and eternal spirit so that my life will be transformed by the God within me.

I am led by my soul's fullest expression and vision for my life.

The peace and presence of God reacts to every condition in my life, and it allows me to become aware that good will emerge from all circumstances.

Below is a mantra from the Bodhisattva of Buddhism.

Om Mani Padme Hum

It is said that all the teaching of Buddha are contained in this mantra. Loosely translated, this mantra means "finding the jewel in the thousand-petal lotus" or "hail the jewel in the lotus." The mantra is used in meditation, but it can be practiced and affirmed to center your mind as well. Tibetan Buddhists believe that by saying the mantra to oneself invokes the benevolent attention and blessings of Chenrezig, who is the embodiment of compassion and attempts to deliver all beings from suffering. You can also just say *Om*, which is regarded as the syllable of the supreme Reality. It is used as a word of invocation and adoration. It is a symbol that represents the manifest and unmanifest aspects of God. You can quietly say this to bring you back to the moment when you find yourself ruminating in negative thoughts and emotions.

Have you ever prayed for God to let you see yourself the way He sees you or to know yourself as He knows you? Through visualizations and affirmations you can receive. This will bring us to Prayer and Meditation..

Prayer and Meditation

> Prayer is not asking. It is a longing of the soul. It is daily admissions of one's weakness. It is better in prayer to have a heart without words than words without a heart. —Mahatma Ghandi

Many of us pray in different ways. I don't believe there is a right or wrong way to pray. Simply stated, prayer is often described as us talking to God. However, when we encounter a struggle in life, many of us either turn away from God and prayer or we seek out ways to become closer to God through prayer. Prayer and the choice to pray are personal experiences. During grief, it is normal to feel disconnected from God and self. The reason for this is because we experience ourselves and God through the relationships we have with others. When a person close to us dies, the sensory capacity we have used to understand ourselves and God has shifted. At first, the shift is so uncomfortable that we are reluctant to move with the change, so we resist it. Some stay here for a bit, then the resistance becomes so gripping that it forces us to fall back into life. It is usually at this point when prayer and meditation finds us. While we are here on the earth, we need to be connected to God, ourselves, and each other. It is an intricate part of the healing process.

Prayer requires that your heart be open, cleansed, and pure before God. The scripture Mark 11:25 says, "But when you are praying, first forgive anyone you are holding a grudge against, so that your Father in heaven will forgive your sins, too." Your willingness to offer forgiveness for any offense or pain that another has brought to your heart will allow you to turn to God with a sincere and faithful heart. Any obstacles such as offense and unforgiveness are stumbling blocks in prayer. You are essentially blocking the transmission of giving or receiving an effective prayer when your heart is filled with grievances. You might say "well, this person doesn't deserve forgiveness" or "you don't know what they did to me." While all that may be how you feel, the only person you are hurting is you.

So, how many times will you allow others to continue to hurt you? Holding on to offense is like saying you hurt me so now I will continue to hurt myself just so I can get you back. It doesn't really make sense. Forgiveness is a gift you give yourself, and it allows God to move through your life with grace and love. You may even find a place in your heart where you can offer a prayer for those who have hurt you and let God show them the error of their ways. It is not our calling in life to hold others accountable for their behavior. We are only accountable for our own. When you turn to God, search your heart for the ways in which you might need forgiveness so that God can begin to work in and through you. Sometimes the hardest person to forgive is yourself. You can beat yourself with destructive self talk that says "how could I allow someone to treat me like that?" or "how I could I have let this happen?" When you fault, blame, and shame yourself away from God, it helps to know that God forgives you and once forgiven you can forgive others. Through prayer, you open the gates to forgiveness and find yourself walking on the path of healing, hope, and restoration.

When you pray, it is important to understand why you pray. Is your prayer a list of things you need or want? It doesn't have to be only materialistic things sometimes a prayer for help with patience could be the same as a prayer for a Lamborghini. If there is a lack of understanding, both can seem meaningless. Truthfully, all prayer is meaningful if it is given with graciousness and a loving heart. Many of us think we really know what we need and want, and so we go to God telling him our requests. The truth is no one really knows what is best for them, whether it be good or bad, because every experience in life is an opportunity for the soul to grow and remember itself. We are able to know pieces of truth while we are here on earth. The complete truth will reveal itself when we are no longer in our body but in the spirit because we are eternal beings. So there may only be some partial understanding now as to why this or that happened or maybe no understanding at all. Some things are not meant for us to know here and now.

Prayer requires that you trust in God enough to know that all our questions in life may not have answers. Psalms 139:6 says, "Your infinite knowledge is too wonderful for me; it is high above me, I cannot reach it." Yet, through prayer there is an understanding that speaks to the heart. The quiet peace of the heart is the language of prayer. Prayer aligns our being with the inner knowing from the divine and its truth. When I pray, I always know that I am seeking God, but I always feel like spirit is seeking me first. I always feel like God is asking me to dig deeper and to give something spirit can work with. When I do this, I discover that it is never about the words or the request but it is about searching the soul for the truth in whatever the situation may be.

Somehow, I knew this when I was younger, even though there was pain back then, too. I never stopped praying throughout my life. Maybe this is true for you too. If you are a younger person, stay connected to your truth and try not to let negative emotions dictate your thoughts. Prayer is an important part of the healing process, and it becomes a greater force in life when it is combined with other practices such as visualizations, affirmations, and especially meditation. It is important to remember that life can weaken us but prayer strengthens us, no matter what our age. God is not waiting for an eloquent speech, supernatural ability, or tests of our memorization skills, but God is waiting for you to give your heart a voice. God listens to the silent voice within you.

Sometimes we may not have the words to express our soul's yearnings. The spirit offers prayer for us. Romans 8:26 says, "So too the Holy Spirit comes to our aid and bears up our weakness; for we do not know what to pray to offer nor how to offer it worthily as we ought but the Spirit himself goes to meet our supplication and pleads on our behalf with unspeakable yearnings and groanings too deep for utterance." Another interpretation says, "And the Father who knows all hearts knows what the Spirit is saying, for the Spirit pleads for us in harmony with God's own will." (TLB) Search for your prayer that is in your heart, and give it to God. You know it's there, and God knows it's there. Remembering is why you're here. Through a simple and sincere prayer you will encounter God and either gain truth and understanding about life and its circumstances or learn to trust God through the times in life that just don't make sense.

When you pray, you become closer to God. Through prayer there is a divine intimacy or union between you and God. To think too much of yourself during prayer weakens that intimacy. You may turn to God seeking, asking, wanting, and then discover that God is doing the same with you. When you pray, you should think to yourself, "Am I telling God about the things I need or want? Am I praying or complaining?" You wouldn't want the people you loved most in your life to constantly complain to you about everything that is missing in their lives. Yet, this is what some of us do when we pray. God answers prayers, not complaints. A prayer that is effective and from the heart allows God to reach into your soul and show you your truth. The soul's awareness is the path to God.

Let's say your prayer is for something very personal and meaningful like "God, why did this have to happen in my life? I can't do this anymore. Please take away this pain and sorrow I'm feeling right now." This may sound like a prayer of despair but God hears your heart and feels your pain and hears it as a prayer for hope. As you continue to search deep down in your soul you can ask spirit for help. You may ask, "What is it I really am praying for here?" God invites you to try again and you offer the same prayer, "God, I can't do this, please take away this pain and sorrow." But God can't take away something that you are not willing to give up. You can now pray a prayer of surrender. To surrender your cares to God doesn't only mean "to give up" it also means "to give to." There is a place where you can pray, "God, I surrender, or give, this pain and sorrow to you." And then you can search your soul for its prayer. You may offer a prayer something like this:

God, I don't know why things happen as they do. I pray for peace in my heart and for my loved one to be at peace. Thank you for holding us both in your loving care. I give all this pain to you God. Take it from me God. I pray to honor my loved one's life by living with love. God, teach me how to love through a broken heart and fill this place inside of me with spirit so I will never lose myself or love again. I know that so much good came from my loved one's life, and that good is still here with me now. I know that you were with them, you are with me, and we are all here now. Thank you for allowing their life to touch mine. God, let your strength and grace show me the way from here. Amen.

Obviously, your prayer will be more intimate since it will be your own journey to your soul. After praying something like this, you will begin to see changes in your life. It may seem like when you pray this way that you are talking to God, but the truth is that God is talking *through* you. Jesus teaches His followers how to pray in the Bible through the scripture in Matthew 6: 7–15 where it says, "And when you pray, do not keep on babbling like pagans, for they think they will be heard because of their many words. Do not be like them, for your Father knows what you need before you ask him." That is the beauty of a soulful prayer. Your prayers are God waiting to meet you or you encountering your Higher Self. Through prayer, God becomes one with your heart and soul. God knows what you need, and prayer will allow you to receive the spiritual unity and power of God through all your circumstances. Each time you pray you move closer and closer to truth. You will be guided not only through the day but in your prayers for the day as well. This is where you will discover that your persistent seeking of God sustains you through life. The union of the Spirit in prayer joins your divine prayer with God's divine plan for your life, which is your plan in truth. Life becomes perfect through the imperfect when we are one with the thoughts of God throughout the fragile moments of life.

The most important aspect of prayer is making it a way of life. It is more than just words—it is a way of being. You are a living prayer. You are alive with power, light, and love. Wherever you go, God goes too. Consider your prayers as being the thoughts of your day. When you are going about your routine either at home or at work or with friends and family, let God be a part of it all. Share your day with God. Remember God as you are doing and living your life. Trust that your thoughts, words, actions, heart, and every aspect of your being are all expressions of God's love individualized as a prayer from the mind of God moving through you at every moment. This is the eternal prayer as eternity prays through you. And always be thankful to God that this is so.

Messaging a Prayer

If you are finding it difficult to find the words to get closer to God in prayer, just try a simple writing activity, which is an introduction the Messaging Process. Writing helps to filter your thoughts for clarity. Think about whatever you may need prayer for, and ask God to show you guidance. As you begin to write, you will know if the words are coming from your soul or your mind, because an effective prayer will emerge only if your soul, or God, is sending it through you. You will know it is effective when the words and its message are authentic and meaningful. Just sit quietly and write the thoughts that flow from your heart. Allow God to use your hand to pen a prayer for you. Think to yourself: if God were here, what would be said to you about this circumstance. Then, be present with this thought, and let your soul speak its truth. An intimate, authentic prayer will be a message from God that only can be revealed to you once you are open and ready to receive. "Let go and Let God" as you listen for the whisperings within your soul.

When you pray, you listen and speak from your heart. In this place there are no insulting words or hurtful remarks. Anything of this nature comes from the mind and the sensory self. It is separate from spirit. You are not listening to your heart if any pain is surfacing. Please sit quietly, and just be still for a moment. Do not force yourself to write if you are not feeling comfortable. It is perfectly normal to retreat from this and return at a time that is better for you. If you decide to stay with it, your heart will open itself up to you and you will hear love, pure love.

When I listen from my heart, I hear the peaceful eloquence of eternal spirit. A gentle inner knowing guides my thoughts, and my heart becomes attuned to a higher frequency. It is not a pitch or sound that I encounter. I just know (or intuit) that I am channeling a greater source than my human capabilities could ever allow. I am listening to a higher presence, and I am comfortable with everything that is coming forth, because it is coming to me in truth. How do I know it is true? I am not left questioning, wondering, or doubting. Truth resonates with your heart. So when you listen with your heart, listen for beauty, listen for strength, listen for love, listen for everything you are in the divine, and you will hear the inner life of your being.

I am sharing a personal prayer message of my own for you to better understand. I began writing and listening to my soul and here is what unfolded.

The "To" Message—This is the first thought you feel. For this purpose it is your first prayer that you give to God. I have been praying this prayer since I began doing the work of writing several years ago. Here is my prayer "God, Let these words and this process help someone, somewhere." As I thought about my prayer, I felt like my soul had a message from God, and so it did and I received the message below.

The "Dear" Message—With my eyes closed and heart open I received this message:

Dear Debra, It already has. The messages, the work you do, this whole process is healing you. I have given you this work to bring healing to your heart. Because your heart is so open, you have become an instrument for healing.

My God Prayer—And so, God led me to pray:

My Dearest God, only you know the purest way to heal a hurting heart. Thank you for your love and goodness toward me and for continually healing me and showing me how much you care. As an instrument for healing I put my strength and hope in you. I place my heart and the hearts of all who grieve into the heart of your compassionate spirit. Thank you for the gift of healing. Amen.

It seems that God could heal the whole world from pain and sorrow in an instant, yet Spirit comes to each of us individually. God doesn't want you to suffer, yet suffering exists. I can't say that I know the reason why suffering is a part of the universal consciousness, and I don't claim to have any answers. Yet, you can recognize this compassionate spirit because it is with you when you cry and when you laugh and especially when you pray. It is with you when others come to your aid either through a friend, doctor, or rescue worker, and in many other ways. It is always giving.

The infinite spirit of God loves you so much that it individualizes itself for the sake of comforting, loving, and healing you through others as well as within yourself. Healing allows you to see that God's true image for you is to have peace, love, comfort—and yes, joy. Yet, for most of us, the only way we can remember this about God is through suffering. This is the greatest message of healing. Healing is God telling you, "Stop suffering. Just be with Me; know Me; remember Me."

This is not to say that there will never be suffering in life again. Often, the spirit of God usually awakens in our consciousness through an intense period of suffering in life. Pain, both emotional and physical, is a very real human experience, and it exists from the aspect of the personal, sensory self of our being, which separates us from God. It is through healing that one returns to God again. The manifested God suffered and died for the love of all His sons and daughters through the crucifixion of Jesus Christ. A unification to God was offered through the crucifixion. With that same love, God is with us through our own trials and suffering as we come into union with this Divine Spirit. It may be that suffering allows the soul to see its highest good for this life and for the eternal life of the indomitable spirit when it is faced with dignity and grace. But for whatever reason why suffering is here, it helps to know that God is in the midst of it all and transformation is possible when this spirit is present. While you are experiencing this sorrow, think about meeting God half way every day. When God makes the choice to want to be known by you, it will happen and then you will discover "The peace of God that transcends all understanding. His peace will guard your heart and mind in Christ Jesus. You will learn to be content with this earthly lot, of whatever sort that is." —Philippians 4:7. This is the tranquil state of the soul as it moves toward union with God.

So, how do we get to the point where we become so close to God that Spirit can talk through us? By making contact with God. This will bring us to Meditation.

Meditation

> Where is that moon that never rises or sets? Where is the soul that is neither with nor without us? Don't say it is either here nor there. All creation is Him but for the eyes that can see. —Rumi (Sufi Poet)

Meditation allows a person to naturally be in contact and control over oneself by withdrawing the five senses and the functions of the mind from the outside world and focusing toward the inner dwelling of one's mind or God Self. In this place, all the negative thought patterns of the mind or personal subconscious are diffused into positive patterns by the healing energy of God. When you meditate you come in contact with God. Meditation is contemplation. You are attuning your mind to spirit. Meditation allows you to integrate the contact you have made with higher states of spiritual consciousness into conscious daily life and positive behaviors toward yourself and others. It is in making contact with the ultimate nature of God that you experience your true reality.

God is not a man with a beard who sits in a big fancy chair in the sky. The presence of God and light are within you. Through meditation, you allow for this light from within to illuminate the world around you. In the Bible, Jesus refers to this spirit place within you and around you in Luke 17:20–21:"Asked by the Pharisees when the Kingdom of God would come, he replied to them by saying, The kingdom of God does not come with signs to be observed or visible display, Nor will people say, Look! Here! or See There! (because it will not be visible to the world), For the Kingdom of God is within you and among you."

Jesus called this place the "Kingdom of God," but he could have easily called it the "Kingdom of Love." Through meditation, you come in touch with the presence of God, which is the eternal love that is within you and all around you. When you go within, you are never without. Within you exists the eternal spirit, guide, counselor, love, peace, and healer.

If prayer is God talking through you, then meditation is God talking to you and you listening. Meditation allows God's thoughts to be impressed upon you. The God thoughts in you begin to surge through to your subconscious and conscious mind. This is the purest way to pray. You develop an inner knowing that is trusting, creative, intuitive, loving, joyful, and confident. It is through meditation that we commune with the nature of God.

Jesus said, "But when you pray, go into your room, close the door and pray to your Father, who is unseen. Then your Father, who sees what is done in secret, will reward you. And when you pray, do not keep on babbling like pagans, for they think they will be heard because of their many words. Do not be like them, for your Father knows what you need before you ask him."

Jesus said this as a reference to meditation. You will discover the secret place of prayer that Jesus is referring to through meditation as a state of consciousness within you. He is telling you to close the door to the outer world and enter the upper room of consciousness, or higher places of inner awareness, where there is union with God. With meditation the natural senses of the self become enhanced with inner spiritual guidance. Jesus is saying to go within to the secret, quiet place of your soul and you will be rewarded with wisdom and revelation to meet your needs because God knows of your needs before you ask. The "asking" is your journey to the silent place of your inner life where you can commune with the divine to receive its understanding for your outer life.

Then, with this inner knowledge, you can manifest the desires of your heart, if they be your desires in truth. The asking is an inward search for wisdom and God. With meditation God will allow you to see yourself and know yourself as God sees and knows you. God will allow you to see and know others as God sees and knows others. Also, God will allow you the grace and peace to see your circumstances with eternal hope. Your eyes will be opened to see the divine in every situation.

Through meditation you are under the influence of God. When you meditate, you are essentially praying because you are aligning yourself with God consciousness. This consciousness will allow for a pray, God's prayer, to come forth through your meditation. You will begin to have an inner knowing of clarity and truth moving in your life. You will know that you were created with a unique set of talents, abilities, and personal qualities so that you can co-create with God and serve with your gifts. Through this inner knowing, you come into union with the "all knowing" God of your being. To have the wisdom to know your divine gifts and then lovingly serve with the gifts that God has given to you for their highest good will allow you to have fulfillment and peace in your soul and in all areas of life.

As long as we are human, we will always feel the need to ask because we think we know what we really need in some way (just as Jesus said "they think they will be heard because of their many words"). The truth is that everything we really need is all divinely within us here and now. Psalms 51:6 says, "Behold, You desire truth in the inner being; make me therefore to know wisdom in my inmost heart."

Meditation aligns you with God so that your prayers are centered on the truth in your soul. Then, your prayers are answered according to God's individual expression for your soul. So, in some way, your prayers are always answered, but it maybe not be in the way you think they should be answered. This is all difficult for human limitations to grasp, and so the practice of meditation is necessary for praying and discovering your own God prayer or your prayer for truth from the quiet place of consciousness.

In meditation, your answers do not come through with any special messages that you can hear. Actually, through meditation you come in touch with complete *silence*. There is nothing that speaks as loud as the voice of silence. Through the breath of meditation, you hear the profound whisper of silence as the voice of God. This is your encounter with God. It is the stillness, the peace, the unity of silence that allows God's nature to be imparted to you. You are listening for the ways of being like God when you meditate. This seems strange to listen for ways, but the listening leads to a knowing. The inner knowing from silence will bring you in contact with God and divine revelation. The silence becomes music for the soul and spirit. There is a wisdom teaching that says, "From the enlightenment of music comes the wisdom of…silence." Let the melody of silence reign over your mind and move your being with the rhythms of God. God's wisdom will be your song.

Most people think when you meditate you are in an inactive state of awareness. Actually, the opposite is true. During meditation, you should be very alert and aware not only to your inner world but to your outer world as well. If you are meditating with your eyes closed and someone walks into the room, you should be aware of their presence.

Meditation is a practice of heightening your inner senses not dulling them into a sleepy state of consciousness. Meditation tranquilizes the mind. Some may fall asleep during or after meditation because they are so relaxed and tranquil. Although this is acceptable, your focus should always be on remaining alert, aware, and attuned to your inner and outer surroundings to receive the greatest benefits from the practice of meditating.

Meditation doesn't require thought—it requires your alert state of being. During meditation, you are being with the presence of peace, light and love. These ways of being will permeate your mind and allow you to relax and let go. Before meditating it is important to relax and pace your breathing. Consider using the same breathing sequence that you used during your visualization. You can attune your senses by closing your eyes and allowing all the sounds around you to be present. As you hear them, just be with the sounds and don't label them. For instance, if you hear an ambulance going by, try not to let your mind define the noise, just hear it and let it pass. Do this with all the sounds and thoughts as well. As you continue to listen with your eyes closed, the sounds and thoughts will become less obvious and you will begin to attune yourself to the silence of your inner being. The silence will seem to melt away the sounds. As the sounds and thoughts move through you try to be present with them and allow them to pass by with gratitude.

Eventually, you will feel a stillness within and all around you —stillness and silence that are aware and alert. It is in this union of the both places where you contact Divine Presence from within. The nature of God, or primal energy (the energy of first cause, first creation of God or Christ light energy), is an all knowing, ever present state of consciousness and being. It is the presence of God light that you have come in contact with during meditation.

The same is true when you are stressed with emotions or thought. The same practice of allowing them to pass, just as you did with the sounds, can be applied here. The key is not to label anything; just be with them and take a moment to close your eyes and let them pass through you. Let the God light change and attune your thoughts. The beauty of meditation is that it only takes a simple moment to return to truth and silence and remember the God within. In doing so, your outer world will come into alignment with your inner world.

You can consider doing this practice of meditation for a few moments right now:

Sit up with a straight spine in your chair with your feet flat on the floor or ankles crossed, each hand placed on your thigh with palms up toward the heavens. Begin with closing your eyes and withdrawing your outer senses inward to your inner senses. While you eyes are closed, you may see colors. This is fine. You are looking into the majestic life of your inner being. If you see an inner light, focus on the light through your inner sight. Allow your inner sight to focus on the colors of light from the interior part of your forehead. Remain with your eyes closed and slowly breathe. See the light moving within and all around you. You are covered and protected by a shield of white light encircling you. Listen to your breath. As you inhale, feel as though you are breathing in peace, and as you exhale, feel the release of all that is not peace. Let your breath carry away the thoughts in your mind, and let the sounds from the outer world pass you by as you allow yourself to melt away into the silence of the divine. You are quiet, calm, and peaceful. The silence and light are moving through your being and purifying your soul. Just quietly breathe and relax. You are being with peace, love, and silence. You are with God. All is well and good. Enjoy the splendor of this intimate moment with God. When you are ready, slowly open your eyes to the outer world. Bring your hands in prayer position and fold them to your heart center. There is peace above you, peace below you, peace around you, and peace within you. Look around at your surroundings now. Ahh! Everything appears more beautiful and alive. You are refreshed.

You can do this for a few moments every day. Eventually, you will find yourself feeling more comfortable and relaxed. When this happens, you may find that when you open your eyes from meditating the moments have passed so quickly because you were not aware of time and space when you were in your inner meditation world. You will notice changes within your being and life just by taking a few moments to connect to God each day.

The Bible teaches that we should have the heart of a child when turning to God. Just as the Christ child is born anew within us each Christmas, meditation allows for this child spirit to be within you each time you withdraw from the happenings of the outer world and enter into your quiet inner life, the manger of the heart. You will encounter the spirit that is within and infinitely beyond you. Meditation allows for this child-like nature to unfold because we are just being with God. There are no words, no expectations. There is only love, gratitude, and even joy. More importantly there is peace. Psalms 46:10 says "Be still and know that I am God." The stillness of meditation allows you to experience the presence and peace of God. It is here, as a beloved child, that you become an open channel to receive when this is your nature.

In Luke 18:17, Jesus says, "I tell you the truth, anyone who will not receive the kingdom of God like a little child will never enter it." A little child receives with trust, gratitude, innocence, and joy. Through meditation you are connecting with God within you. The kingdom of God is found in your higher state of being and your awareness to the presence of God. Jesus referred to this of place of inner being in the Bible scripture Matthew 6:33, where He said, "But seek first the kingdom of God and His righteousness, and all these things shall be added to you." It means to have joy and peace here with you now in all you do and with all you love.

Discovering the kingdom God within you is your gracious reward for seeking God first and foremost in your life. As Jesus said in Matthew 7:7, "Ask, and it will be given to you; seek, and you will find; knock, and it will be opened to you," which refers to you knocking on and opening the door of consciousness through meditation and discovering your divinity as you seek to become the recipient of infinite wisdom.

When you seek you shall find, and you will be amazed of the treasures that dwell within you.

Be excited! You may feel like not much is happening, but remember, you must release your expectations and all desire for outcomes when you meditate, because meditation is about the present. It is about the moment, the now. You are spending time with God, dropping in for a visit, so to speak.

Once you enter into meditation like this, God can impress the gift of higher thought upon you. For example, divine inner presence will guide you in your life, even with your prayers. You may find yourself going through a normal day when you feel something inside you prompt you to think about someone, a friend or relative, and you take a moment to call or pray for them. You don't know why, and more importantly you don't need to know why, you just know that you should either call them or pray. This is a God thought moving through you. Your meditation practice has opened your mind to receive this thought. Or maybe you have not been able to resolve a difficult situation in your life, then suddenly, a solution or "soulution" comes to mind. Another God thought you have received! Through your presence with God and meditation you are receiving presents. You are becoming one with the mind of God. There are so many ways meditation can allow for you to become an intuitive channel to receive inspired and spiritual guidance in your life, especially toward healing. Be open, trust, and receive your gifts like a child—with joy!

Different people enjoy different ways to meditate, depending on their own personal preferences. In John14:2 Jesus says, "In my Father's house there are many dwelling places. If it were not so, I would not have told you; for I am going to prepare a place for you." Jesus is telling us that we are multidimensional beings with many levels of consciousness. Through meditation you can discover the dwelling place within you that is one with God in the unconscious mind. The consistent practice of meditation will allow you to ascend to a higher state of consciousness within the deeper levels of your subconscious mind so that you can dwell in the heavenly place of your being. Meditation allows you to enter into the heavenly realms of consciousness that exist within you.

There are many different practices of meditation. Here is a brief overview of some meditation practices that you may implement in your life so that you can allow for the deeper levels of your being to come into contact with and release the God light within you.

One practice is called Meditation through contact or contemplation, which is what I've described and implemented above. This is when you sit quietly and come in touch with the inner life of your being. This is your holy place. It is your sacred encounter with the presence of the divine and inner splendor. Another practice for meditation is called Affirmation Meditation. In this practice you deliberately drop positive affirmations into your consciousness by either reading them to yourself or saying them out loud. You would do this slowly and intentionally focusing your mind on the affirmation and feeling the positive energy of the words. This meditation might be described as positive thought affirmation process. You can consider using any of the affirmations that are listed in this book or any of your own. Another meditation is a Walking Meditation, which is when you consciously use your senses to become completely aware of the steps you're taking and your surroundings. Again, you would not label or define anything you notice. You are just observing and becoming aware through mental alertness.

Also, you can attain presence through awareness by utilizing a practice of seeing things around you as if you are seeing them for the first time. You can find something to focus on and look at it as if you have never seen it before. There aren't known names or words to describe these things because this is your first experience of it. If a thought about the object pops into your mind, allow it to be there and let it pass. To just be with nature or a part of your surroundings in this way is a powerful way to become present. I would like to take this a step further and share another way to attain presence which is by looking at your life around you as if you would never see or be with it again. To observe the moments with gratitude because you know that each one is not to be taken for granted. To look and be with your life and the people you love in your life in this way offers great appreciation and love for them and everything you have, because the breath of life and the people in it are the gifts of every moment.

This is what it means to be with the concept "live like you're dying," which is a popular phrase in our culture today. Although this is not a typical meditation practice, I wanted to share it with you because taking a moment to do this helps to bring me back to a place of gratitude when I feel like I need to remember what is truly important in life. I'm sure you have done this before many times yourself. It allows for you to keep your priorities in the right place. Meditation doesn't have to be complicated. Any practice that allows you to remember love, gratitude, and peace is bringing you in contact with the divine energy of God within you. Through meditation and becoming present with awareness you allow for the beautiful gifts in every moment to unfold all around you.

There are many other meditations, and you can consider finding places that offer classes to instruct and guide you through meditations as well. If this is your first time practicing any meditations, I would recommend considering having another person present with you before you begin any meditation practice for your own comfort if you desire. Meditation should always be a relaxing and pleasant experience. It offers great benefits toward healing your life.

Chapter 4

The Messaging Process

Creativity is the power to connect the seemingly unconnected.
—William Plomer

Introduction to the Messaging Process

> Have faith in him at all times, you people; pour out your hearts before him: God is our safe place.—Psalms 62:8

There are many paths in life. All paths, especially the spiritual paths that lead to God, are good, because they are led by the One Spirit that is guiding each of us individually. When a soul is ready to receive truth, Spirit seems to find the way. Sometimes a path seems to unfold as an answer to a higher calling that has come about through the trials and difficulty encountered in life. For me , I found my path, or I should say, my path found me, from a place within my soul that I thought I had lost. I had always loved writing but I never thought of it as a way to make a living, especially not in this way. And this is a strange way to describe the writing that I have done because that is exactly what it did for me—it gave me a living, not through monetary support, but through the birth of the words for Heavenly Messages~ Forever In My Heart I found my life again.

Through the rhyming pattern of each message a rhythm entered my life and spirit began to flow through me. Over time felt I myself coming to life. When I first began to write these poetic messages, I had no intention or idea for their purpose. At first, the writing was so intense that I thought that I was going to die and I was leaving behind messages to everyone so that they will know how much I loved them. Then, I realized the perspective of the writing, and I began to write messages more frequently with greater intention and purpose. Most of the writing came through me during a light sleep so I began leaving a notepad at the side of my bed. I would feel the need to write some messages early in the morning, while driving, even in the shower. The feeling to write came about any time and any place, and I was open to receive.

It was as if God had taken hold of me and was telling me what to write and who to write to, but I never was told why I was writing. I felt as if I were channeling heartfelt thoughts and emotions of grieving hearts everywhere. God was using my broken heart for a greater purpose, and within every piece of its brokenness I was given a glimpse of each of you.

Then, one day, my husband and I went to visit our loved ones at the cemetery. We saw people were leaving behind generic cards to their loved ones covered in plastic. Finally, I understood the purpose for these messages. I realized that this writing experience had expanded my heart toward all of those who mourn. I began to create poetic messages for people to bring to their loved ones who had passed so that they can place these loving thoughts in cemeteries, gardens, or any scared place. I know these words that were given to me healed my life, and I believe they have the power to do the same for you. More importantly, I believe that the process of Messaging offers great healing, because we only truly heal when we allow our hearts to expand and get our minds off of ourselves.

Because grief is a very individual experience and as such it can be very isolating, the Messaging Process provides an opportunity to explore the depths of our heart and soul. It is here where we discover we are not alone. We discover that grief is a universal emotion. As we tap into this emotion and feel its pain for ourselves and for the loss of every other heart, we begin to grow with compassion and empathy. Allowing yourself the time and space to step into another person's heart offers your soul powerful insights about the divine within us all. Once you experience grief from another person's heart, your heart will know oneness, and you will begin to offer them love. When you offer love to another, you receive love back yourself. This is the way healing brings peace and comfort to your heart and soul. Every day, God comes into your heart to heal you. You must be like God and do the same. When you go into to the heart of another you will search your heart as well. You will be healing. Through my own grief, I was extremely depressed and isolated. Through my darkness, God's light magnified a path.

In doing this work, I have met many beautiful and courageous people. I have learned and grown through so many hearts. I can't really say that I can teach anything about grief, because I have needed to learn so much more then I could possibly teach, but I will try. In my attempt to make some sense of it all I have made this effort of writing a book to pull some thoughts and insights together to share with those who may be as lost as I was in grief. What is it they say? we always teach what we need to learn—well, here I am. Grief is not an experience you can master. At least I know this is true for me. I know that each experience of loss crumbled me to my knees, and it would do so again. I would have to learn to heal all over again.

Even Jesus, when he learned of the death of Lazarus, was deeply moved by Mary and Martha's grief and wept with them over their brother's death. So, I guess in some way those who grieve are in good company. Yet, grief is a very powerful experience that removes you from your spiritual center. When you move away move away from your spiritual center a death takes place in your being. Only with truth and love can there be a resurrection to deeper knowing of life. For now, at least, I have learned, and I can share with you that this healing is a moment by moment, breath by breath process.

The way a person grieves depends on the closeness of the relationship with their loved one and the way the passing of their loved one has affected their life. A loved ones passing may be different from person to person, even within families, because of the conditions of the relationships prior to the passing. These conditions may include a particular role you may have had in your loved one's life or your day-to-day interactions with them. Basically, every relationship is different, and your response to the loss of a relationship will depend upon how that person influenced your life. This is why grief is such a personal and often isolating experience. I have learned that each experience with grief and loss tells its own story. Although the loss may be different, the stages, emotions, and movement through grief are the same. Each story is told with different names, circumstances, and events, all masking the universal truth of spirit.

We all will have our death stories that our family members and friends will be left to tell, I will have mine, and you will have yours. But all that remains is the love and passion we brought to this life and the people it touched. This is the beauty of spirit and its infinite presence. Love and spirit live on, and death is not an ending, it is a resurrection to a new form of being. This new form of being, or spirit, exists as a non-physical manifestation of light energy in the state of eternal consciousness. Spirit or consciousness moves your being before you came to this place as well as your physical form while you are manifested on earth. It continues to move as a field of infinite energy once the form is gone. This is a simple understanding of eternity from which there is seemingly no beginning and definitely no end supported by the laws of physics.

Eternity exists within you at this very moment. Therefore, when I think of eternity, I believe it is an instantaneous transfer of pure love to eternal spirit. A merging of the finite and the infinite in one eternal moment where all the love you have ever given and all the love you have ever received are all magnified by the light of God. I believe this is why Jesus said in Matthew 22:37–39, "You shall love the Lord your God with all your heart and with all your soul and with all your mind (intellect).This is the great (most important, principal) and first commandment. And a second is like it: You shall love your neighbor as yourself." The more love you give to others always flows back to you and to God. It is the love you have lived that continues on in your eternity. So it makes perfect sense to live this life with great love and passion. This communion of bountiful, heavenly love is the energy of all that is beautiful and eternal. And you will recognize and remember all the faces of love once your infinite spirit makes its transition to the eternal light of God.

I hope the following brief stories offer you a better understanding of the concept of eternity being within you now. I think of life as being a series of bus rides. There is a journey through every joy, sorrow, event, and relationship in life. So let's begin your bus tour to eternity. For instance, you start a new and fascinating career so you get on board the "career path" bus. Then, you find the person you love and you get married, so you jump on board the "marriage bus." You may decide to start having children and you jump on board the "new family bus." Then, there are the sorrowful journeys, like losing a loved one. You may not jump on board for this ride, but it is a trip that you must take so you take your seat and settle in for a bumpy ride. Then, finally, one day, you're waiting at the bus stop and the sign on the bus reads "Eternity." You know this is your last trip, and you get on your way.

While on this trip, the bus takes you through all the events that you have traveled through in your life. The ride allows you the opportunity to reflect on all the relationships you have experienced. If you were married, then you are able to have a ride through your marriage, and as you do you may think "I could have been a more understanding." Then, you drive through your friendships and you think, "I could have been more giving; I could have had more fun." You may drive through your work place, time spent with your family on holidays, and other occasions, and all your thoughts are "I could have been a better parent, daughter, son, grandparent, lawyer, plumber—basically, I could have been a better person, I could have loved more." You also travel though your sorrowful events, and you think, "That made me so angry and bitter. I hurt myself and so many others. I could have learned so much more."

The bus comes to a stop, and you run up to the driver and ask, "Can I go back?", but the driver offers no answer. As the bus doors squeal open, you turn and begin to walk down the steps and through the doors knowing you could have done better in your life, not only for yourself but for all the people you left behind who never really got the chance to see your true beauty. As your spirit moves ahead there is a bright light, and you recognize it as pure love. The light offers you comfort and holds your spirit in eternal peace.

Or there could be another scenario. You're standing at the bus stop and the bus sign reads "Eternity." You know it is your last trip and you get on your way. While on this trip the bus takes you through all the events you have traveled in your life. The ride allows you the opportunity to reflect on all the relationships you have experienced throughout your life. If you were married or divorced, your bus ride takes you through these events, and you see all the joys and challenges you faced together. You think, "It was work, but it was so worth every moment we shared together. There was so much love between us, whether we stayed together or not."

You take a trip through your friendships, and you think, "Wow, I really enjoyed being with those great people." You even get to see a stranger you smiled and said hello to in the park one afternoon, and you feel good about that moment too. You have the chance to visit the years past and see your parents, who may have passed away many years before, and you feel the precious joy for having had lived the life you were given. You drive by, taking in every sight and memory. Then, you see yourself as a parent, and you think, "I was so blessed to have these beautiful children share their lives with me—I love them forever." All these moments spent with your children flash before you, and the energy of their laughter becomes a whirlwind of musical sound that lifts your spirit as you soar with love toward your heavenly destination.

As your spirit continues to travel, you are given the chance to reflect on the time spent with family during special occasions and holidays, and you see all the joy you spent together. Even though there may have been some challenges now and then, they were always resolved and forgiven, and so you smile for the journey. You then travel through your sorrowful events, and you think, "Oh, how that hurt me. I thought I would never get through. I grew so much and became so strong. Look, there I am actually helping someone else through their pain. I would have never thought I could do that. Life is amazing." Your spirit continues on the ride, and you see yourself as a child, worker, sibling, as a human being, and you know that you gave all you could to everyone and did your best throughout your life. You are eternally grateful for the beautiful gift of life and all the relationships and experiences it allowed for you to know and to love.

The bus comes to a stop. You make your way to the front, and before you step off the bus, you turn to the bus driver and say, "Thanks for the ride." The driver graciously acknowledges as he tips his hat and sends you on your way. There is something familiar about this driver, and then you recognize that the driver is the spirit of God within you, accompanying and guiding your finite life into your infinite existence. The bus doors squeal open, and there is a brilliant bright light. You recognize and intimately know the light as pure love, and your spirit is embraced with this union. You now see all the love you have ever given and all the love you have ever received. It is all there waiting your arrival. Your spirit is radiant. You are in Paradise.

So now, I guess the question is, "Where would your final destination be?" Whatever you are now, you will be forever and ever through eternity. Your state of consciousness at this moment will carry you to the eternal moment. So, it is vital to your finite and infinite life that you currently maintain a healthy, positive, loving, peaceful existence. Every person and every event in your life is your opportunity to experience the love of God and your truest self. The best news is that if you are not living your best life you have the power to change your life and create Paradise here, within you now and for eternity. You can love on purpose until your purpose becomes love. You have a responsibility to yourself and to your loved ones to leave the best of you behind and then to bring it all with you as well. Live your life with love, through every event, toward yourself, and with every person, and you will have the ride of your life!

There is a quote that I love which says, "They say that when you die your life passes before your eyes. Make it worth watching." Your life could be the greatest love story you'll ever see!

The Heavenly Messages, which I have written, are in some way like stories, because each one touches on the illusion of emotion and then leads us to our eternal truth, which is love. I call these emotions illusions because they are just that—they are the distractions of our personal selfhood. These feelings of depression, isolation, and self-punishing pain are our own attempts to hide us from our truth. This keeps us separate from God and love. However, these emotional feelings are a very real part of the human experience. These feelings are actually the aspect of our being that makes us human. At times, if only for a brief moment, while an emotional reaction is taking place in reaction to a challenging circumstance in life, you may feel a silent sense of composure, or maybe a sense of calm, that sweeps over your being.

This sense of calm is connecting you to your God experience. You are not feeling separate from God when this feeling is present with you. Creation manifests itself through the illusion of being separate from God, which is what makes us all look and act differently from one another. However, we are all different pieces of the same pie. We are all expressions of One Spirit. God is the ultimate storyteller of our being. We are free to act out our roles as we wish as long as in the end we all graciously remember to take a bow with the One Divine Intelligence who has created the script. The overwhelming thoughts of sorrow and pain that completely disconnect the spirit from truth create the most challenging roles for us to play, yet it is here where we remember God. The experience is given so that ultimate truth can reveal itself to us.

So, what is ultimate truth? I can only share what I know to be true for my heart. If what is shared resonates with your heart, then it is true for you too. Our physical form is only here on this earth plane for a period of time, some longer than others, but still a finite number of years. Bur we are eternal spirit, and each of us leaves an imprint of spirit upon creation and the hearts and souls of all we love; the definition of soul can be given as person's mind, will, and emotions. You can call it your personality or a place within ourselves where our personal sense of selfhood is individualized and aligned with the consciousness of God.

So, spirit lives in our hearts and can move through our mind, will, and emotions. Spirit moves the soul. But we can lose touch with spirit when negative layers of thoughts and emotions cover the heart and soul. This makes us forget our true being. The purpose of healing is to align your soul with spirit. Healing ensures that you are not being ruled by negative emotions of the personal self but by the nature and spirit of

God. All these negative thoughts are the functions of the lower mind, and they cause the soul to live in darkness because the mind has essentially switched off the light. The light is still there but it will only shine when the mind is switched to operate on a higher energy of consciousness.

The passage from St. Paul that says "Let the mind be in you as it were in Christ Jesus" helps to understand that there is a battle of the mind that exists in all of us and we must be diligent in discerning the ways to overcome. You must align yourself with God to have the mind of Christ. To be aligned with God means to renew your mind every day according to God with the ways and thoughts of God or Higher Consciousness. You can do this by saying positive spiritual/universal affirmations or scriptures from the Bible as well as other spiritual practices such as meditation/visualizations and prayer. This allows a Christed mind to be with you as you heal. You can choose to operate in the functions of the mind, flesh, or personal self or in the functions of the spirit, heart, or authentic self.

Heaven or hell exist within you and are created through the power of a single thought. Heaven is within you as your state of unity, eternal love, and your connection to divine spirit. Hell is within you as your state of isolation and fear, and is disconnected from divine spirit. Whichever exists as the inner life of your being will be a mirror reflection of your outer world. I refer to heaven and hell as states of the mind to allow for an understanding of the peace or torment that can exist within. Heaven and hell should not to be confused with religious connotations of these words. Obviously, your religion will have its own meaningful expression of heaven or hell. There are many different views and beliefs in regard to these terms. I only offer these terms as words that are references to states of emotional beingness.

Your thoughts have the ability to create higher or lower states of consciousness in your soul. When you are aware of your thoughts, feelings, and emotions, you enable yourself to merge with higher levels of consciousness, which can elevate your mind and allow for a heavenly way of being to exist within you. To be aware or to have awareness means to have a knowledge of the presence of God with you; it means to be one with God in your soul. In the book of Job from the Bible, Job says it this way, "I know my Redeemer and Vindicator lives," Job 19:25. Job was a prosperous man who suffered many trials in his life. He had lost his health, all of his possessions were taken away, he lost his cattle, servants, and a terrible tornado destroyed his home killing all of his children because they had gathered there to find shelter. But with Job's faith through the long suffering, God allowed Job to regain his health and have seven more sons and daughters, he gained back twice as many cattle as he had before, and he lived another one hundred and forty years. No matter what you think or feel about your circumstances you must know, as Job knew, that God can turn it around. Now that's awareness!

Awareness is your willingness to believe that there is a higher consciousness within you that is greater than any of the ruminating thoughts of negativity and pain. This higher consciousness is greater than any circumstance that you are currently facing in your life. A willingness to believe like this requires faith. There is a beautiful quote that says, "A little faith can bring your soul to heaven, but a lot of faith can bring heaven to your soul." This is what it takes to allow heaven to exist within you—the kind of faith that knows that God within you lives.

The healing, love, wisdom, and all the revelation you seek are in you through the spirit of God. This means as you move, God moves. You may find yourself talking to someone who has had a similar experience as you that can offer you healing. The fact that you are reading this book allows you to know that God is moving through you and has pointed you in the direction of this book. If you find that this book doesn't help you, then you will continue to be guided to another book, person, or place and most importantly, back to the inner life within you, the God who is your redeemer and vindicator who lives in you. You might say, "But I am still feeling pain and sorrow." Yes, but trust that as you keep knowing the truth and love that lives in your heart and applying the ways of God to your life you are healing. Spirit can never be broken or apart from you. It is always alive and giving. Therefore, it is imperative to be diligent in becoming aware and observing your thoughts and how they are making you feel and react so that you can operate in faith and respond with wisdom to function with well being throughout your life. This will make God operate your hands, feet and your entire being so that the spirit of healing can manifest in your life. To walk through all the challenges in life without human frailty is a great gift from healing. All of this will guide you to the peace in your soul.

With grief, when the mind, will, and emotions are not guided by the spirit, the soul will try to wrap itself around the concept of the death experience. When this happens, our mind, will, thoughts, emotions, or our soul, becomes frayed and are misaligned with the consciousness of God. The light has been turned off and disconnected. It is important to manage all the aspects of our being and be led by spirit. Only with spirit, which resides in the heart and manifests through our being, can our souls find the peaceful state of consciousness as the heaven within us, the eternal light.

Our truth is that we are spiritual beings living out a physical form. Our spiritual nature exists within and infinitely beyond us through the oneness of creation. We are all created of one spirit, and one multiplied by itself is always one; it never equals zero or nothing. One spirit multiplied by one spirit, over and over, remains one, eternally. When someone dies they remain with the One Spirit or God of perpetual life. Naturally, when someone we love passes we will feel and have very real emotions of separation, which in terms of grieving are normal aspects of the healing process since our emotions serve as guides uniting us toward our one truth. However, when these emotions and thoughts become severe and begin to thwart your life and darken the soul you become lost, broken hearted, and disconnected from your divine truth. Your heart has been covered and forgotten when the One Spirit who lovingly created you is separate from your being. This is when you need to search the depths of your heart. You need to remember all that is eternally yours and connect to God, which is the Truth or Divinity that manifests itself though all existence and physical form.

Ultimate truth is your knowing of the divine within. It is your union with God. This awakening of consciousness allows you to become one with the ultimate truth of your being and the guardian of your soul. It allows you to connect to the infinite spirit within and beyond you, so the light of heaven can meet earth each day with eternal love. In Colossians 3:12, it says that you must "Clothe yourselves therefore, as God's own chosen ones, His own picked representatives, who are purified and holy and well-beloved by God Himself, by putting on behavior marked by tenderhearted pity and mercy, kind feeling, a lowly opinion of yourselves, gentle ways, and patience, which is tireless and long-suffering, and has the power to endure whatever comes, with good temper. Be gentle and forbearing with one another and, if one has a difference (a grievance or complaint) against another, readily pardoning each other; even as the Lord has freely forgiven you, so must you also forgive. And above all these put on love and enfold yourselves with the bond of perfectness which binds everything together completely in ideal harmony". In other words you must choose or carefully select your behavior toward your circumstances and not allow your feelings and emotions to dictate your life. Only spirit can offer you the ability to choose to over ride your emotions with your divine inner strength and truth by uncovering your heart and listening to your spirit. The Messaging Process that you are about to discover and explore in this book will allow you to begin your search for truth as you enter into your heart and soul to journey on your spiritual path toward healing from grief.

Let's move on to the Messaging Process so you can get on your way toward healing.

The Fifteen-Day Journey toward Spiritual Healing from Grief

> Give sorrow words; the grief that does not speak whispers the o'er-fraught heart and bids it break. —William Shakespeare

Many of us are familiar with journaling as a process of exploring the unconscious mind through writing by free association. This allows our emotions to spill out thoughts and cover the pages with words to express our feelings. Your emotions in grief surface as a way to heal you. The word emotion comes from the Latin root which means "to move through or out." It has been said that E-motion is energy in motion. The Messaging Process is much like journaling but it allows you to tap into the energy that moves you through grief so that you can gain a sense of freedom. The word freedom is derived from the German word *Friede,* which means peace.

Messaging will also allow you to write out automatically all the negative thoughts that are in your mind, just like journaling. However, the difference is that once these thoughts have left your head you will continue to write from the eternal place of your heart to renew your mind. You will begin to notice your thoughts shift toward love and peace. Once this occurs, your words will begin to coincide with your positive thoughts. You begin to see and feel a transformation take place from within you and on the page.

The Messaging Process engages your own creativity, because it allows you to respond to your thoughts, feelings, and emotions by letting your gifts of the spirit live through you. Your intuitive guidance and inspired knowing will move you beyond your intellect to a place of higher thought. You create by the awareness of your inner presence to the divine that is moving and unfolding everything in your life moment by moment. When you tap into this awareness, you authentically relate to yourself and connect with spirit.

The Messaging Process is a creative way to cleanse and purify the soul. Through the creative process of writing and spiritual practices you have read about in this book you will pave a path toward healing from grief. Messaging is a fifteen-day process of reaching within to the depths of your inner self to overcome the gripping emotions of grief with truth and love toward yourself and others. Through a series of messages, or I should say "To" and "Dear" letters, you will be exploring your thoughts, feelings, and emotions with spirit as your guide. Your "To" letter will be your opportunity to express all your thoughts, feelings, and emotions. You can be very expressive here.

I can tell you that I had no problem writing my "To" letters and expressing my emotions. Many years ago, I was a young girl from Brooklyn, New York, who needed to write out everything I was feeling about pain, and all I can say is I had a way with words that wasn't too enlightened. I didn't know that God was preparing me back then to create a Messaging Process, but I did know that whatever was inside of me was way too painful to keep. I had to get it out of me, and writing was the only way I knew how. I have been messaging about life's challenges and grief since then. So don't be shy, write all the pain and hurt out of your being. Remember, you are detoxifying. This is your cleansing process.

Then, you will write your "Dear" message. This message will be a divine message that only the truth in your heart can deliver to you. This is your purification. As you cleanse and detoxify the thoughts of intense sorrow and pain you will need to replace your spirit system with healthy, life-giving thoughts of love and hope. Through this process you will heal and expand your heart. Your capacity to love yourself and others will overflow with understanding and compassion. It will guide you to discover the infinite that exists within you and everyone else.

Since the Messaging Process is a fifteen-day activity, you must be willing to commit to do this for a full fifteen days without missing a day. *I also strongly suggest that you commit to another fifteen days once you have completed the process.* I recommend this because research has been done to support the notion that a healthy, healing pattern can materialize in a person's life within thirty to forty days of a change in behavior.

You will allow yourself to receive the most benefits from this process when you do it day by day with commitment and love. You owe this to yourself, so take the time to begin to heal. There is no greater gift you can give to you. You should set aside a time of day that is best for you. Some prefer the morning time because they feel there is an interrupted sense of consciousness that offers a steady stream of thought during the earlier hours of the day. Yet, some have a better flow of thought in afternoon or in the evening before bed time. Please commit to which ever time of the day that works best for you as you begin the process.

At times I will be sharing some short examples of messages to give you an idea of the process, but do not allow these thoughts to interfere with your thoughts. The process begins slowly as to not overwhelm you, but you will be moving through many of your emotions and thoughts day by day. As you move further through the process there will be questions to guide your writing for the Messaging Process. This is your experience, so please embrace the process and engage yourself in the experience.

Also, please keep in mind that while you are writing your messages and once they have been written you should not edit by adding thoughts to your messages or by taking thoughts out of your messages or worry about grammar. This will disrupt your thoughts and block the flow of writing as it comes through to you. Your words will surface as they should, so you need not concern yourself with editing. No one will see this but you, so no worries about what or how you write. This is your healing journey, your time for you. This activity will offer you inspiration and allow you to immerse yourself further into the healing journey. You will be writing two messages a day, maybe more some days, and at the end of each day of messaging, there will be a metaphysical activity to culminate your experience.

You will need a pen and lots of paper (maybe a notebook or journal), a quiet, peaceful space for writing, and an open heart. Please make sure you are comfortable by adjusting the light and temperature in the room to your preferences. Also, consider the room and space where your writing will be taking place each day and try to let it be comfortable and organized. Before you begin, you can consider lighting a candle with fragrance such as rose or sandalwood or any other scent that may be pleasing to you to offer peace and calm to your surroundings. As you light the candle, take a moment to look at the candle's glow and see it as a portal to the infinite where you can align and release your intentions for your writing each day so that you can move with the flow of consciousness. Try to make your writing place inspiring and serene.

It is also important for you to please remember to keep each of your day's work as you move through the process. You can consider using a folder to hold all your letters. Your emotions, thoughts, and feelings are all your guests, some may be unexpected and not wanted, be gracious to all since they each come bearing gifts. Welcome to your healing journey.

You will begin every day of the Messaging Process with the spiritual practices or techniques of visualization, affirmation, prayer and meditation. Below is an overview of the techniques that will assist you as you begin:

Affirmations—You will begin each day of your Messaging Process with affirmations. Consider choosing five affirmative statements that resonate with your spirit. Say these statements slowly, intentionally, and repetitively each day. Feel the positive energy moving through your being. These affirmations are empowering and healing you.

Prayer—After you affirm your positive statements, consider sitting quietly and praying your "God Prayer." Pray this prayer from your heart with love and gratitude as it was given to you with the same.

Visualization and Meditation—Before visualizing or meditating, it is important to consider the breathing and other suggestions offered to you from the" Spiritual Path Toward Healing" chapter in this book. There are two practices to consider:

You can do the visualization and the meditation from the chapter in this book called "A Spiritual Path toward Healing" or you can blend the visualization and meditation. You can consider doing this. You can consider meditating for a few moments right now:

Sit up with a straight spine in your chair with your feet flat on the floor or ankles crossed, each hand placed on your thighs with palms up toward the heavens. Close your eyes and center on the light that is within and all around you. You will focus on this light at the interior region of your forehead. You will visualize the light moving from the crown of your head, throughout your body, to the soles of your feet. As it moves through your being, you feel the warmth of light balancing your body, mind and spirit.

The light is touching and healing the nucleus of every cell in your body. The light is purifying your thoughts and energizing your spirit. You are becoming absorbed in the glow of healing light. The white light holds the energy of all the rays of the color spectrum. A mosaic of pure color essence is now within and all around you. The white light permeates through the rays of color to illuminate your inner being. You feel the majesty and beauty of this Holy Place. Your inner light is radiant. You are imbued with pure white light. The light is like a blanket covering you. You are protected, safe, calm, and peaceful. You are loved.

You now allow yourself to dissolve into the tranquility of your inner being. You focus your mind on the white light of God. As the light unifies your heart with spirit and love you are calm and peaceful, yet alert and aware. You remain here quietly until you gently bring your senses back to the outer world around you. You slowly open your eyes and stretch your hands up to the heavens and then bring them toward your heart center and fold them in a prayer position to your chest. You are grateful, peaceful, and spiritual. There is light above you, light below you, light around you, and light within you. All is well.

Once you become familiar with this visualization/meditation you consider replacing the word "you" with "I" or "my. You will do all of these techniques each day before you begin your Messaging. The Messaging Process will pace you through your healing journey every day. As you move forward, you will gain awareness and awaken to your truth. Your commitment to the process will allow for this experience to support your healing. You are now ready to begin the Messaging Process and the healing journey. All my love and prayers are with you.

The Guest House

This being human is a guest house.
Every morning a new arrival.

A joy, a depression, a meanness,
some momentary awareness comes
As an unexpected visitor.

Welcome and entertain them all!
Even if they're a crowd of sorrows,
who violently sweep your house
empty of its furniture,
still treat each guest honorably.
He may be clearing you out
for some new delight.

The dark thought, the shame, the malice,
meet them at the door laughing,
and invite them in.

Be grateful for whoever comes,
because each has been sent
as a guide from beyond.

Rumi- Sufi Poet

The Messaging Process—Journey Within to Find Your Heaven

Days One through Fifteen—a day-to-day writing process that will cleanse and purify your soul as you move through grief.

Day 1

Welcome to your first day of your healing journey. You will write a "To" letter and a "Dear" letter. Your first day of the process will allow you to confront Death. Yes, that's right; you are writing a letter to Death and then a letter from Death. In your "To" letter you are not searching for fancy words or thinking about your grammar. There is no editing, revising, or anything that can filter the flow of emotion. You are writing from the inner flow of pain that is eating away at you. Let all the words come out of you. Tell Death exactly how you feel. Feel free to express in any way that you want. This is your time to say whatever you feel. You will not come back to this to add or edit anything, so be as open and expressive as you possibly can.

Here is a short example; you may write something like,

Death, you suck! You ruined my life, my family, everything I knew, and everything that was beautiful, you took it away when my father died. I am so angry that I have to live the rest of my life without my Dad. Not only am I suffering but my mother is always crying and my whole family is devastated. I feel so alone. From Kathy

You see how this is going. You will continue to write like this until all your feelings and emotions are exposed and thrown outside of you on to the paper. Remember, don't be shy. You are here to detoxify and cleanse all of the pain from your heart, mind, will, and emotions. You are cleansing your heart and spirit. Give your thoughts and feelings about death a voice. You have a right to feel this way. Express it here and now. Once you have written all of your thoughts down, you will stop and take a moment to be with your feelings. Close your eyes and take a moment to breathe and relax. You are calm, safe and peaceful.

Open your eyes, be still and quiet. When you are ready you can move on to the "Dear" Letter.

The" Dear" letter always comes from the same place as your "God Prayer" in every message you write. The "Dear" letter is a message that only God can send through your spirit. It is a message of pure truth and love. The "Dear" letter allows for you to purify your being with truth from the divine within you. To write a message from death you have to think from the perspective of God. You have to use your divine vision to see the higher meaning from this experience. You can go back and read your "To" letter. Consider searching within to find any speck of light in this darkness. This is your opportunity to give spirit a voice. You will be surprised at what death can reveal to you. Ask God, "If death has any kind of message for me, what would it be?" If you feel like you're not getting an answer, ask again. Keep searching for the truth underneath the mask of death.

Here is a short example of a "Dear" letter:

Dear Kathy, I know how hurt you are, and I am sorry. I didn't come into your life to destroy it. I wonder if you ever really noticed your mother with such love before now. It seems like your heart is growing. Your life be can't be ruined when you still have so much love in it. If I hadn't come into your life, you wouldn't know this kind of compassion. Don't take the moments for granted. All the love that made life beautiful is still there, in you. It may feel different but it's the same love as before. You are here to recognize it.

Your message will be from your own God voice within you. Listen closely, and receive this powerful gift of truth from your soul. Now ask yourself, "Am I willing to accept this message death has revealed to me into my life?" Your willingness will open your heart to receive this truth.

Once you have written your own letter from death and received its message, you can consider closing the process with a silent moment of prayer to offer gratitude for your divine message. Spend some time reading the message quietly to yourself. Allow the words from your inner voice to permeate your soul. Close your eyes and sit quietly for a few moments. Release all your thoughts and just be. You are with God, love, and spirit. You are calm, safe, and refreshed. When you are ready, open your eyes. Consider closing the process with your God Prayer.

You have accomplished a great deal today on the spiritual path toward healing. The following activity will assist you toward integrating your work today with the healing process.

Activity: Choose a day this week, preferably today, to take the time to sit and watch the sunset. Allow yourself to be very present with the experience. Notice the magnificent colors as the sun ends its work for the day. It seems as if it is at its most glorious time during sunset. Once the sun goes down, the day will be done and never to come back again, yet, the sun gracefully fades into the horizon knowing that creation holds its palate and brush for the sun to rise with the dawn of morning. Only you see the sun that has gone away, but creation allows for the sun to shine in another place while you wait for its return. The sun never leaves; it is just somewhere else giving light. Although the form of day is finished as you may know it, the sun's perpetual light shines even when the sky is dark. Allow the setting sun to be your hope for perpetual light, and know that light is always shining even when you don't see it.

Day 2

Please have your pen and paper ready. Find a comfortable and quiet place to relax and to write. You will begin the Messaging Process with your affirmations, your God prayer, and your visualization/meditation. Once you have spiritually aligned yourself with these practices, you are ready to begin. Today you will be exploring your emotions. You will choose one emotion from grief that you feel is gripping your life at this time right now. Consider the stages of grief and try to explore which stage is relevant to your emotions right now. You will write to this emotion and from this emotion. All your emotions are here to tell you something, and this process is going to allow you to hear what they are saying to you.

It is understandable if you feel like you have more than one emotion present, but for today, you are going to use your inner laser sight to target only one emotion. You will be writing to your various emotions throughout the fifteen days, so it would be helpful as you move through this process to choose the one that is giving you the most difficulty for each day. And if this emotion continues to surface, you will be able to confront it again. You will write directly from the emotion itself. You are expressing in your letter to the emotion how it makes you feel, what it is doing to your life, and the life of those around you. Any feeling that you can intuit about this emotion, you will express it through a message.

Let's continue with the previous example from Kathy, who experienced the loss of her father. In a brief example she writes"

To Anger: You make me feel like I have a beast inside of me. I don't feel like I am the same anymore. You make me push everyone away, because I don't want to be close to anyone again. The world looks different to me now. It doesn't feel safe to me because things can change so fast. I am angry that my father died and left us all to take care of ourselves. I am angry at people who say they understand but they really don't. I'm angry because I don't know how to feel right now. Anger makes me lost.

You can see how Kathy is experiencing anger as she write the "To" letter to this emotion. As you write, you will continue to express more than this in your letter. You must be very present and aware of the emotion to speak to it in this way. All your thoughts are rooted in your emotions, and if you believe these emotional thoughts, you can't heal. This is why you must be able to identify the one emotion that is pressing on you the most right now and confront it. This is your chance to come face to face with an enemy from within. Write it all out on to the page and release the poison that is destroying your life.

After you have written your "To" letter to your emotion, it is important to bring yourself back to a place of gentle calm by closing your eyes and taking a few deep breaths. This will help to relax you.

You have allowed a lot of pain to surface and move through you, so you need to take some time now to sit quietly and be comfortable. Every time you write a message that is revealing your hurt, you must always take the time to relax and recharge.

Now, you can return to the process with ease and begin the "Dear" letter. The toxicity you have just released must be replenished with proactive thoughts of truth and love. The "Dear" letter is your inner guidance translating the language of your emotional pain to you so that you can understand it and have a peaceful relationship with it. It is your soul's voice of spirit as you begin to hear your message in truth.

For example, Kathy's "Dear" letter offered her this message:

Dear Kathy: It must be so scary to feel like you have a beast inside you and to not feel safe in your world. You must know that I am here in your life as anger because you are afraid. You fear to love people because you think they may die and leave you. You fear that with your father gone you won't be able to survive. Because you are so afraid, you are lost. Your fear is making you feel me, your anger. Don't be afraid. You are loved and safe. The only way to overcome fear is with love. You have to replace all the feelings I am giving you with love. It is so much easier right now to be with me as anger than to be with love. Just flip me, your anger, over to love for yourself and everyone in your life, especially your Dad and all this will go away. Always know that when you can't find your love and truth anger shows up in your life. I am here to help you find what you lost. Your friend, Anger.

It is now your turn to receive your God message from within you. Listen closely and hear the truth of your soul speak to you. Then ask yourself, "Am I willing to accept this message into my life?" Your willingness will open your heart to receive this truth.

Once you have written your own letter from an emotion and received its message, you can consider closing the process with a silent moment of prayer to offer gratitude for your divine message. Take a moment to read the "Dear" letter that your inner being as sent to you today from this emotion. Let this divine message sweep over your soul and cleanse this pain from your being. Then consider closing the process with gratitude and your God Prayer. Your spiritual path toward healing is moving forward every day. You did a lot of inner work today, so consider doing the following activity to integrate your healing process.

Activity: Listen to instrumental music that is inspiring and peaceful. As the music plays, light a white candle for purification, and as you light the candle affirm the following statement, "I send all negative thought and energy into the light." Allow these words, the glow of the candle, and the soothing music to bring energy of calm, ease, and love within and all around you. All is well.

Day 3

Welcome. This day will be a very important day in your healing journey as you move along with this process. Be ready to begin your Messaging Process by having a pen and paper (journal or notebook) ready and go to a quiet, peaceful place to write. Your writing space should be neat and uncluttered, and the temperature and scent of the area should be comfortable and pleasing. Today, you will be writing a "To" letter to your closest loved one who has passed and a "Dear" letter back. The "closest loved one who has passed" refers to the passing of someone who was an integral part of your life, a person who shared moments with you each day.

If the death experience you are currently facing is both your most recent and closest loved one, then you will write to that person. If you have recently experienced the death of another loved one as well as the passing of a loved one in the past, decide which is the closest and most hurtful loss in your life and write to that loved one first. You will have another opportunity to write to your loved ones again so don't feel like you are choosing one experience over the other. It is just that for today your writing will have greater healing if you confront the death experience that has been most difficult for you.

Please allow some time before Messaging Process to center yourself with your affirmations, your God prayer, and your visualizations/

meditations. Once you have aligned yourself with spirit you are ready to begin the process for today. Your "To" letter to your loved one who has passed will be a letter that expresses all your feelings, thoughts, and emotions about your life the way it was when they were alive and also about your life the way it is now. You will write about all the joy you felt from their life when they were here and about all the sadness you feel now without them. You will tell them all that is in your heart. Your "To" letter is your chance to say the words that were left unspoken or to write the lingering thoughts of the words that were left unwritten. You are here today without coincidence. Use this moment to express the inner most yearning of your soul to your loved one. They are here with you now; they are listening.

I will not offer you an example because you intuitively know how to do this. This message must come from you to your loved one without any outside interference or assistance. This is your journey, where the finite meets the infinite. Explore your heart and soul and write, write, write. Your heart wants so much to speak, let the words flow from your awareness of spirit and love. And know with every ounce of your being that every word or thought you express have all been here waiting for this moment to come, you are here now. Let your heart have its voice.

You will begin with, "To..."

Now that you have written your letter to your loved one, you will allow yourself the time and space to be present with all your thoughts and feelings. You will close your eyes and gently return to your inner light. You are calm, peaceful, and loving right now. You are grateful for this moment. You are quiet, peaceful, and comfortable. As you begin to open your eyes, you feel refreshed and relaxed.

You are now ready to receive your "Dear" message from your loved one. Your heart is open and your soul is willing to express spirit through you. You are listening from your divine inner presence that is your connection to the light from God within. This is your time to open up to where the eternal exits and to dwell within its infinite love. Just as your moment to write your "To" letter was ready and waiting for you to appear, so has this moment been here awaiting your arrival. There are so many beautiful, loving thoughts that your loved one has been wanting to share with you, and now they can allow for these words to be present through your loving and open heart. Your experience with your "Dear" letter will allow you to discover the truth of eternal love and spirit that is always present within you. Your heart will serve as the tool for encountering and expressing all the inspiration that your loved one can share with you from beyond. You are one with eternity, so let the eternal speak and send through you its message for healing. This message is only for you from your loved one. Your message will allow you to understand and accept your life as it is now, because love guides the heart to truth.

Once again, I will not be sharing an example for a "Dear" letter because you intuitively know your divine voice from within and any outside interference will disrupt your ability to receive. This is your healing journey and your healing message. This is your time to be with spirit and your loved one. During your message, you will feel the love and beauty of your loved one and their presence within and around you. This is a sacred moment—a moment of inner spiritual unity. There are no words to define this; only the experience can speak for itself. At this time, allow yourself to be an open, clear channel of love, and let the words pour from your heart on to the paper. You are writing from a pure stream of consciousness. As the words find your hand, allow yourself to be present with the process. Your awareness will create the truest reality for your message to come forth. Know that your loved one has been waiting to share this time with you. Your message is from them through you so that you will experience truth and love, forever, in your heart where they will always be. They are here in spirit with you now, listen to your heart. You will begin to message with, "Dear..."

Now that you have received your "Dear" message, you will read it quietly to yourself and allow the love and inspiration of this moment to wash over your entire being. You are feeling loved, connected, and peaceful. You have so much gratitude toward your loved one for allowing you to see the truth beyond this momentary place of existence and for sharing this divine message with you. You are awake, aware, and alive. Love is eternal. Consider closing this experience with your God prayer.

Today, you have embraced your healing journey with grace and love. You have welcomed spirit into your heart. Consider doing the following activity to integrate and honor your experience for today.

Activity: One day this week, perhaps tomorrow, wake up early and watch the sunrise. Be present with the moment as you begin to see the sun cover the sky with its abundant light. Only creation can effortlessly manifest the awesome splendor of a new dawn as its light breaks through the dark night to illuminate the day. Allow God's sunrise to be your light through your darkest hour. Let creation radiate your hope for the light to shine throughout eternity. Know that every day eternal light shines on you and your loved one; you are both one with the spirit who has given you this miraculous gift.

Day 4

We will continue on the healing journey and explore another emotion today. Take time to align yourself spiritually with your affirmations, your God prayer, and your visualization/meditation. Be sure you are prepared to begin your writing for today. Also, find a place that is comfortable and relaxing. Are you ready? Let's move on.

There are many feelings surfacing within you today because of your emotional activity yesterday. Healing is an ever present force in our life because it only takes one memory to bring back all the emotions that we thought were healed. Healing allows us to heal, over and over again; our hope is that with each opportunity to heal we are more aware and maybe a bit wiser. Nonetheless, as the opportunity presents itself, there are choices you have to make. You can choose to deal with what you're feeling or choose to ignore it. You may think, well, if I ignore it, it will go away. When you do nothing and ignore your feelings, you are actively making a choice, even though it appears as though you're not. The choice to do nothing is the same as the choice to do something. So consider making an active choice to do the thing that will help you to heal, which is dealing with your feelings. You are the only one who can save yourself. You are coming to your own emotional rescue with this process. Although you may feel different emotions present with you right now, you will use your inner laser sight to find the one emotion that is most intense at this moment.

Keep in mind, that all the emotions of grief come and go without sequence. There is no order to the emotions of grief. So, for instance, you could be feeling like you are dealing with denial right now. Even though it may be years since the loss, the emotion of denial may be present with you. The same is true for all the other emotions that define the stages of grief. Your emotions don't know about time—they only know what your brain is telling them. This is your battle—it is in your mind, and you have to stand up against the enemy. Decide which emotion is most fierce within you right now, and destroy it.

Let's look at brief examples of the "To" and "Dear" letters for today. We will look at the emotion of denial, for example:

To Denial: It is so difficult for me to grasp that I will never see or talk to my loved one again. Why do I have to go through all this and even try to understand this experience? It is just too painful. I would rather stay in denial. Denial helps me to forget all of this. I don't want to remember what I've lost. I don't want to deal with this at all. From, Paul.

Your "To" letter to your emotion will be in more detail, and you will express more about the feelings associated with your emotion. Just write whatever thought comes to mind. The secret to overcoming difficult emotions is to confront them and get rid of them through writing. You are purging yourself in this process, so allow it all to come out of you. Once you have written your letter to your emotion take a few moments to stop and unwind. Be aware of your feelings right now. Know that you are calm, safe, and at ease with your surroundings right now. Take a few healthy and strong deep breaths. As you breathe in think to yourself *I am breathing in peace and love.* As you breathe out think to yourself, *I am releasing all thoughts that do not serve for my greater good.* You are replacing all the toxic thoughts with pure and truthful thoughts.

Now that you feel comfortable, you can move on to the "Dear" letter. In your "Dear" letter you have to use your divine, inner scope to navigate the higher meaning for denial. Every emotion is here to tell you something about yourself that you need to know. Emotions serve with great intention when we become aware and open to receive. Write out an answer to the following question, "What is it that this emotion is guiding me to know in my life?"

For example, the "Dear" letter may return a message like this:

Dear Paul: I know I have made you feel comfortable by allowing you to not face your life and your loss. But this kind of comfort will only bring you more pain. You will never begin to heal if you don't allow this loss in your life to become a part of you now. Acting like it never happened does not take the pain away— you're just avoiding it, and as long as you do I will have to continue to show up and push your reality away. I am here for you to know that once you embrace what your life is right now, you will become alive again. Don't deny your life a chance to live. Let me help you live your life in truth. Your friend, Denial.

It is now your turn to receive your God message from within you. Listen closely and hear the truth of your soul speak to you. Then ask yourself, "Am I willing to accept this information into my life?" Your willingness will open your heart to receive this truth.

Once you have written your own letter to your emotion and received its message, you can consider closing the process with a silent moment of prayer to offer gratitude for your divine message. Then consider closing the process with a moment to read your message, quiet contemplation, and your God Prayer. Your spiritual path toward healing is moving forward every day. You are making great strides in your healing process. Remember, this is not a destination, healing is a journey. Consider doing the following activity to integrate your healing process.

Activity: Allow yourself some alone time and soak in a warm, relaxing tub. If you would like to synergize your bath time with your senses, consider pouring in three drops of essential lavender oil. Lavender is known to cleanse and soothe the spirit, which results in a calmer approach to life. This is your time to revitalize from the day. It doesn't matter if you are female or male, anyone can benefit from this experience. Enjoy and relax—you deserve it!

Days Five–Twelve

For the next eight days your messaging will be focused on your loved ones who have passed and your emotions. Let me explain how this is different. On Days Five and Six, you will be messaging to your loved ones who have passed. On Days Seven and Eight, you will be writing to and from your emotions. Then, on Days Nine and Ten, you will be messaging from the heart. Finally, on Days Eleven and Twelve, you will write to and from your emotions for the last time. This is an intense writing period. It will really allow you to cleanse and release all the emotions, feelings, and thoughts associated with these experiences as well as expand your heart with compassion.

There are some people who have experienced more than one loss in their life time. If this is you, then you will be able to draw from those experiences for the Messaging Process. The twist to this process that really promotes healing involves a technique that will allow you to get your mind off of your own loss by stepping into the grief experience of another or messaging from the heart. This aspect of messaging allows you to write from the hurting heart of another person who has experienced loss so that you can get your mind off your own grief and learn that you are not alone in your sorrow. This will allow a space for healing to enter your heart.

So, you can see it doesn't matter whether or not you have had many experiences with death or only one, the healing process will be the same because you will be messaging through the heart of another person. For example, if you are someone who has experienced the passing of a young teenage niece or nephew you will message to and from that loved one as you have done previously. It is beyond words to express the tragedy of losing a young life, yet it is only through a writing process that allows you to purge your thoughts with words that the loss can begin to move toward some kind of a healing place.

Once you have done your "To" and "Dear" letters, the next day you will take this experience a step further. You may tragically have lost a niece or nephew but your brother or sister lost a child. In this step, you will message from their heart to their child and back from their child to them. You might say this is too depressing—why would I do this? Well, the truth is death is depressing, but the only way to begin healing is to see the experience through all eyes. You will only get a glimpse of their pain. The purpose for messaging from their heart isn't to experience their pain but to expand your heart. You will never understand the loss of a child from this process, but at least your heart will become open to offering compassion where it is needed.

The same can be applied if you lost your father. You will message to and from your loved one, but then you will go a step further and message from the perspective of his wife, your mother. If your mother has passed, then message from the perspective of your father's brother, sister, or friend. Consider someone other than you to get an understanding how this loss has affected them as well.

Yet another way to apply this is for those who have lost a child. Most would agree that there is no greater loss than this in life. The way to message though this grief is to try to see the experience of loss from another parent perspective of someone who has lost either a young child, a child that is teenage to young adult, or an adult child, whichever one is different from your loss. Allowing yourself to view the loss from the heart of other parents who have also experienced the passing of a child at various stages of a child's life will offer you some kind of healing. You will allow yourself to know that you are not alone in your grief and gain greater awareness toward each experience as being different yet the same.

Every loss is unique and it is this uniqueness that allows the grief process to become so isolating. Once you begin to do this process, the isolation vanishes because you see that grief hurts every heart. Even though you may be aware of the hurt, when you write from the heart of another person the hurt becomes unified. You are not only aware of the hurt, but you become aware of the oneness of grief. This will elevate the consciousness of grief with heartfelt compassion, love, and unity. If this seems like too much to comprehend, don't worry. The days ahead will unfold as spirit guides you. Be open and willing to explore the process. This will make sense to you as you move through it. Let's move on to your next day.

Day 5

Welcome again. We will continue on the healing journey and travel a different path today. A journey of the soul embraces all the roads to healing. Allow yourself to be present with this activity for today as you visit to an unknown yet familiar place. Take time to align yourself spiritually with your affirmations, your God prayer, and your visualization/meditation. Be sure you are prepared to begin your writing for today. Also, find a place that is comfortable and relaxing.

Today, you will be messaging from the heart of spirit itself. On Day 3 of your journey you messaged to and from your closest loved one who has passed. Today, you think about your loved one and the other people in their life, besides yourself, who were affected by their death. Let's refer back to Kathy, the young woman who messaged about the loss of her dad. If she were going to begin this process today, her thoughts would have to be focusing on the people who are grieving with her during this time. These people would be his wife (her mother), his children (her brothers and sisters), his mother and father (her grandparents), his brothers and sisters (her aunts and uncles) other family members and her father's friends.

You can see that Kathy has an expansive selection of people to choose from as she begins her writing for today. Someone from this group of people will become "one" with Kathy's heart today. The person she selects will be the person that Kathy feels was also close to her dad: she has chosen her mother. Now Kathy has to consider all the thoughts, feelings, and emotions that her mother may be experiencing during the loss of her husband. Kathy intuitively knows that her mother is feeling lonely, sad, depressed, and afraid, feelings quite similar to her own.

Now, you will do the same as Kathy and think about your loved one who has passed and then consider the other people who were hurt and affected by this experience. You can make a list of names if you need to. Now you have to decide who may have been the closest to your loved one and step into their heart for the moment. Once you are in that place, you will allow yourself to feel their hurt, thoughts, emotions, and feelings. You are becoming one with them in this grief experience.

You are ready to begin to message your "To'" letter from another heart through your heart. For example, if Kathy were ready to step into her mother's heart and begin her "To" message, she would write something like this:

To My Husband: I miss you so much. I miss your voice, your touch, your love. I don't know how to move forward without you. My whole life was you and the kids. Without you, it all is incomplete. All the plans we shared for our future are gone forever. Everything died with you that day. Help me to be strong. I am here alone now. We all still needed you. I don't know how to go on from here. I Love you. Your wife, Pam".

Once this message has been written from the heart of another you will become more sympathetic and the attention of grief will fall from you toward another. Although you may have been aware of feeling sympathy, opening your heart in this way will move you toward empathy and allow you to change your awareness of thought into action. You may begin to offer love in a more compassionate way when your heart is attuned to another person's pain. Once you have written your "To" letter, take some time to sit quietly for a few moments. Let yourself have a silent moment and slowly breathe in through your nose with a count of eight and release your breath through your mouth with a count of eight. Do this three times. You are relaxed, calm, and loving. You are at ease with the moment and moving with the flow. You are healing, and you are peaceful.

You are now ready to move on to the "Dear" letter. This message will allow you to experience the oneness of spirit. For this activity with your "Dear" letter, spirit will be communicating your message through the universal heart of love. You are becoming one with the heart beat of God—the one rhythm that is beating every heart. Through this vibration, your message will be given to you. Be open and willing to receive. You must align yourself to your loved one and the truth in their heart and spirit. Spirit is always loving, giving, and present. Love is eternal. These truths will guide you as you write. If Kathy was going to write her "Dear" message from her father to her mother, she would write something like this:

My Dear Pam: I know how much you miss me. Please know that I am with you, only in a different way. Search for me in your heart. I am here waiting. I feel your love with me here, and I have a part of you and the kids with me always. Please keep a piece of me there with all of you, and don't let sadness and pain take love away. I want you to live your life. I want you to be happy. Those may have been our dreams for the future, but now it is your life that can see it through. Don't let it slip away. Live, love and please laugh. You are so strong Pam. You were always my strength. Live your life and be happy. That is all I ever wanted for you, and I still do. I am with you. I love you forever. Your husband, Tom.

Through her heart, Kathy has learned that her mother is as alone and afraid as she is and that her father's spirit is present and strong. Her father wants his wife to be happy and go on with life. This will help Kathy to move on, because it will allow her to respect her mother's life and wishes as she moves forward with her own healing. Also, if Kathy may have been starting to be feeling any negative emotions such as resentment or if she was beginning to having feelings of responsibility toward her mother, this will allow her to release those emotions so she can fully integrate her healing in a positive and productive way.

Your "Dear" letter will offer you a similar experience as you allow the spirit of your loved one to offer a healing message through your heart. Through this activity, your heart and spirit are expanding beyond limits. You are growing, learning, loving, and healing every moment. At this time, consider offering a silent moment of prayer of gratitude for your divine messages. Take a moment to read your "Dear" letter quietly to yourself. Allow this message to purify your soul with its truth from the divine within you. Then ask yourself "Am I willing to get my thoughts off my own sorrow?" Your willingness will expand your heart in truth. Consider closing the process with gratitude and your God Prayer. Your spiritual path toward healing is moving forward every day. You are making great strides in your healing. Consider doing the following activity to integrate your healing process:

Activity: Take some time to be with the person whose heart you messaged from for today. You could tell them how special they are to you or how much you love them, if you are comfortable in doing so. Or you could just talk with them, either by phone or in person, and share some happy memories of your loved one together. More importantly, be there for them and offer your shoulder to lean on—after all, it was through their heart that your heart beat for today.

Day 6

This is a new day to walk the healing path together. You are doing so well and moving forward with great success. Allow yourself to appreciate the time you have spent doing this work and your willingness to take the journey. I am so proud of all you've done and thankful that you are back here today. Let's begin. Take time to align yourself spiritually with your affirmations, your God prayer, and your visualization/meditation. Be sure you are prepared to begin your writing for today with a pen, paper, or a notebook/journal. Also, find a place that is comfortable and relaxing.

Many people have experienced more than one loss in their life. Therefore, the Messaging Process offers you opportunities to write for those experiences as well. Whether your loved ones' passing was recent or a few years ago is insignificant for the purposes of this activity as you continue through the Messaging Process. Your emotions are not aware of time. A loss that happened when you were a young child can still be present and having a major effect on your life today. Through this process you will confront all those feelings, thoughts, and emotions that you may have pushed aside. These emotions are alive in you and have comprised an aspect of your being that may be difficult for you to recognize because you have suppressed them into your unconscious. Only with awareness lifting these emotions to conscious levels will you allow these emotions to fully integrate. You are bringing light to the darkness, so to speak.

The same is true for a recent loss. If you are avoiding your emotions and masking over them with unhealthy behaviors and attitudes, you will not allow your being to become whole with the grief that is present, and these issues will surface to haunt you in the future. You may think that by not facing your feelings about a recent or past loss that you are or have overcome it, but the truth is you are keeping the pain with you by holding on to the suppressed, unexplored emotional aspect of grief. You have been brought to this path for a reason—allow yourself to be absorbed in this healing process.

Today, you will write to another loved one who has passed. If you have no other loss in your life, you will continue to message from the heart of another person's grief experience. Just as you did yesterday, you will do the same for today. Please refer back to yesterday's process for assistance with your activity today. However, if you have had other loved ones who have passed in your life, then you will draw from those experiences and message to them for today.

You will begin with your "To" letter and write a message to your loved one who has passed. You will express all your thoughts and feelings about the experience and the affect this experience had on your life. If this experience happened some at time in the more distant past, it is important for your healing to explore those feelings now so that you can manage and integrated them into your life in a productive way. Therefore, reflect on that memory and write it out of you in your message. Your message will allow you to rid yourself of all the hurt that has been buried inside of you. For example, if you have experienced the loss of your mother in the past, or even recently, your "To" letter will say something like this:

To Mom: For so long, I haven't been able to accept that you're gone. It is so difficult, especially when I need someone to talk to, someone who can understand and love me like you did. I haven't really let you go, and I don't know if I will ever be ready to accept this. I wish with all my heart that you were here with me still. Mom, I miss you so much. Love you forever, Lisa.

This is a brief example of what your letter will express. You will be writing so that you will release many of the emotions that have been hiding in an unconscious state, and you will make them present. You are here at this place in time to write and release from a steady flow of consciousness and awareness. Do not think about what you are writing—just write. You are not here to judge and analyze your feelings; you are here to rid them from you. *If you feel blocked, then this is your opportunity to know that something profound is just about to appear.*

Don't get frustrated—now more than ever is your time to stay with this process. You don't need to force yourself, but just stay present and ask yourself, "If I knew what I was feeling right now, what would that feeling be?" You intuitively know what you have to write, but sometimes the feelings are so masked that they become difficult to recognize. Be present and open. Allow these feelings to move through you. This is the best part: the feelings that are surfacing are moving out of you. They will no longer be taking up residence inside of you. You are cleaning house and emptying yourself so that you can welcome in a new way of being.

But before we move on to the "Dear" letter, I would like to take a moment to touch again upon the loss of a child. The loss of a child varies with great emotional intensity; therefore, any example I could offer wouldn't suffice in this circumstance. I implore you to take the time to engage in this process and fully write out your emotions so that you can understand how you feel, not change how you feel. Your feelings are here to express through you and make you aware of yourself in life. All your feelings are your true guides and honoring these vital messengers will allow you to come back to you in some way, maybe different from the way you were before, but still you. Embrace this encounter as you heal.

Note! It is important for everyone who is doing this process to know that your feelings are not right or wrong. The Messaging Process is a tool that will assist you in understanding your feelings, not changing them. Validating your feelings through grief is just as significant as becoming aware of them. Your emotions are your keys to the treasure chest of personal growth.

Once you have completed your message to your loved one, please take a moment to relax and breathe. Close your eyes and look within to you place of comfort and peace. You are calm and safe. Allow this divine presence to soothe your body, mind, and spirit. You are one with all that is spirit. For this, you give thanks, and so it is.

Let's move on to the "Dear" letter. The message of the "Dear" letter is to offer you the spiritual presence of truth and love that are still alive within you but may have been silenced through loss and grief. For example, Lisa's message from her mother might say something like this:

My Dear Lisa: I will always love you. I know how much you miss me, but please know that I am still here. Every time you think I am not with you, please look in the mirror, and you will see a part of me looking back at you. You haven't let me go because you can't let go of love. I want you to let go of the pain but hold on to the love. Be joyful and smile for me. My beautiful girl, I love you forever and always. Mom.

Your message will have greater meaning and express much more though you because it will be your very own voice of spirit.

Another brief example I would like to share from the voice of spirit is a message from a child. The spirit of a child holds no gender and is universal in its nature of timeless beauty and love. If a message were to be expressed from a child it might say:

Dear Mom and Dad: I see how much you're hurting. I want for you both to be happy. Remember the way you would always make me laugh and smile whenever I was hurt? I am doing that for you now. I am still with you, so please see me in your life again. I am still here and your heart is with me too. I love you both so much. Mom and Dad, everything is the way it should be. You gave me life. Let it shine in the way you live now. I am always with you. I Love you…

Your divine message from your voice of spirit will speak its truth as it is revealed to you. Allow it to unfold and bring you a message from eternity. Ask yourself "Am I willing to accept this message into my life?" Your willingness will open your heart to receive this truth. At this time, quietly read your message from spirit again to yourself. Consider offering a silent moment of prayer of gratitude for your divine message. Then, consider closing the process with your God Prayer. Your spiritual path toward healing is moving forward every day. You are making great strides in your healing. Consider doing the following activity to integrate your healing process.

Activity: Celebrate and honor the memory of your loved one by preparing their favorite food or meal and sharing it with good family and friends. Or play their favorite song and dance. They are celebrating with you, sharing in these moments. As you allow yourself to enjoy life and smile, they are ever present.

Day 7

Here we are, together again. This will be another day of miracles as the healing process leads you to discover the eternal presence of spirit that abides in your soul. Please take time to align yourself spiritually with your affirmations, your God prayer, and your visualization/meditation. Be sure you are prepared to begin your writing for today with a pen, paper, or a notebook/journal. Also, find a place that is comfortable and relaxing.

For the next two days, you will be writing to and from your emotions. Since you have been working diligently with the Messaging Process and writing to and from your loved ones, you may have many different emotions that are flaring up in you right now. Today, you will examine those feelings. You will have to use your inner laser sight to discover which emotion is most surfacing right now. This can be challenging to do because an emotion is basically a blend of all your thoughts and feelings. Your brain processes more than one reaction to your circumstances at a time. There is an overlap of other emotions with varied levels of intensity that make emotional awareness difficult. It is very important to observe how the emotion is causing you to react. The more you are able to discern the force that is shaping your mental mood and status the better you will be able to manage your behavior.

As you become more emotionally aware through your healing process with grief, you will begin to progress in how you choose to act in the moment. Many of us react to our emotions based on habit, but when you become aware of your emotions you will be able to respond with wisdom or intelligence, instead of impulse. This will allow you to gain control over your circumstances and your life. Each and every time you have feelings that are making you emotional you will take the moment to stop and become aware and ask, "What is this emotion trying to express through me right now? What is it telling me?" As you are scoping through your emotions today, consider which feelings are driving your response mechanisms. Focus on what you are feeling at the moment rather than relying on your memory. This will allow you to better understand your feelings so that you will choose a more positive behavior and reaction.

It is important to remember that your emotions serve as your guides and messengers toward self awareness, but they also offer you protection. Your emotions serve as a way for the subconscious mind to protect the conscious mind. So, when you are feeling anxious, sad, worried, fearful, and so on, always know that this is your subconscious offering you protection from a conscious reality that has been created through your personal sense of selfhood. Through your connection to truth and spirit, you can put your subconscious mind at ease. Every part of you has been designed and created with a divine balance of love and perfection. Always know this is true.

Let's take a look at some emotions and the corresponding behaviors and reactions. This is a list of feelings. For instance, anger can allow all of the following to emerge:[1] outraged, defiant, irritated, hatred, resentful, exasperated, vengeful, belligerent, annoyed, resistant, concerned, and apprehensive. Fear will show itself with the following feelings: nervous, worried, restless, dreading, afraid, edgy, frightened, stressed, overwhelmed, anxious and obsessed.

You can see the variety of ways these emotions express themselves. Read through this list of feelings, and see which ones are surfacing the most today. For the purpose of this activity you will be messaging to two of these feelings for the day. You can do others if you should would like, but really try to find the two emotions that are causing the most difficulty right now and begin your messaging process. You will begin your "To" letter by expressing how these emotions are making you feel by writing down the physical symptoms and emotional experiences. You will also write in your "To" letter all the self talk you tell yourself about what you are experiencing and your reaction to your internal dialogue. The following is a brief example:

To Stress: I am physically drained and exhausted. I can't sleep; my stomach is killing me; I have constant headaches; and I feel like my heart is racing out of my chest. I am withdrawn and sad. You make me say things like "I have no strength to get through this." I will never survive this pain and loss, and I am too weak and too alone. When I say this to myself, I feel like I will never move past this and like I am dead inside. From Pat

---

1 Laura A. Belsten, PhD."Emotional Intelligence Workshop." *Coaching Emotional Intelligence.* Master Certified Coach, Founder, and President of CEO Partnership. CEO Partnership and The Institute for Social and Emotional Intelligence, 2009.

Your letter will be much more expressive than this. You will write all of your thoughts and feelings out of you. This is your detoxification process, so the more you express the more you rid yourself of all the unwanted emotions. Once you have written your "To" letters, take the time to be present in the moment and breathe. You are calm, relaxed, and at ease with the moment. This is a healthy time for you. Sit quietly and close your eyes and enter into you divine presence. Stay here for a bit. When you are comfortable and ready you can move on to the "Dear" letter.

Your "Dear" letters are your opportunity to create a better response for yourself. You will create a response from the awareness you are now experiencing with your emotions. This awareness will allow you to manage your emotions by choosing to respond rather than to react. A *reaction* causes your emotions to rule over your inner and outer world. When you react, you are giving up your control to the emotion. You are putting your emotions in the driver's seat of your life. However, when you respond to your emotions, you are answering with a call of action that is of your preference. A *response* to an emotional experience allows for mental alertness and clarity because you are aware that you have options. You become emotionally empowered when you know you have the option to choose a response that gives you back your control.

Your "Dear" letters will allow you to explore your emotions by offering responses that serve for your highest good. Your letters will assist you recognizing the general spectrum of emotions that are present during a difficult moment. It is in the moment of emotional upheaval when you can choose to respond from your higher emotional self or lower emotional self. You will learn to operate from your strengths not your weaknesses.

Write out an answer to the question, "What is it that this emotion is guiding me to know in my life?" The following brief example of a "Dear" letter can illustrate this further for you.

Dear Pat: I know how weak and hurt you are right now. You feel this pain with such intensity because you have such a sensitive nature. If you allow your sensitivity to draw you in and close you off, I will show up in your life with all the symptoms and feelings that are present now. You will feel stressed and overwhelmed. But I can show you another side of yourself. Use your sensitive side to be kinder to yourself. Allow it to make you become more relaxed, compassionate, and insightful. Let me teach you how to live a better life so that you can understand your life and all its circumstances better. Choose the opposite of stress. I am here to teach you how to relax and accept your life as it is. Sincerely, Stress.

Your letters will be more expressive and provide greater introspection into your emotion. You can see how this letter from stress speaks from a higher sense of self. It allows you to experience the lighter side within the darkness. The following is a list of strengths that will assist you as you write your letter. Consider which strength is serving as your higher emotion at this time.

[2]**List of Strengths:** sensitive, ambitious, compassionate, intuitive, assertive, passionate, thoughtful, nurturing, relaxed, calm, sincere, persevering, humble, brave, logical, stable, balanced, determined, confident, supportive, insightful, patient, considerate, decisive, loving, affectionate, tolerant, kind, sympathetic, understanding, dependable, rational, loyal, open, and caring.

Feel free to add any other words you can think of that may be a strength of yours before you begin to write.

Once you have completed writing your "Dear" letters, offer gratitude for the divine message and the insight you have gained about yourself. Spend a moment to read over the divine message your inner being has sent to you today. Ask yourself, "Am I willing to accept this message into my life?" Your willingness will open your heart to receive this truth. Allow the words to drench your soul with purifying love. Your soul desires to soak up the truth from your inner being today. Please close the process with gratitude and your God Prayer. Your spiritual path toward healing is moving forward every day. You are making great strides in

2 Ibid.

your healing. Consider doing the following activity to integrate your healing process.

Activity: Every time you feel an emotion taking over you, become aware of how you're internally and externally processing this emotion and practice responding from your higher self with strength instead of weakness. Although this may not come easy at first, try setting a reasonable response for yourself, and you will begin to notice a decrease in your emotional stress levels. Consider writing this all down by answering the following questions: What are the weakened emotional feelings you need to notice and pay attention to? What situations and people trigger your weakened emotions? What would you choose as a better and stronger response to find a way to deal with these feelings?

Day 8

Welcome again. Exploration is the essence of the healing journey experience. Today, you will continue to explore your feelings. You will discover a way to implement better strategies for dealing with your emotions with understanding and awareness. Allow yourself to appreciate the time you have spent doing this work and your willingness to take the journey. Once again, I am so proud of all you've done and thankful that you are back here today. You are so strong to commit to this process each day and give yourself time to heal.

Let's begin. Take time to align yourself spiritually with your affirmations, your God prayer, and your visualization/meditation. Be sure you are prepared to begin your writing for today with a pen, paper or a notebook/journal. Also, find a place that is comfortable and relaxing.

Let's begin with the list of feelings and take a look at two other emotions that may be surfacing right now. It is more than likely that during grief you are experiencing disheartening emotions.[3]

3 Ibid.

Disheartened emotions express themselves through the following feelings: weak, impatient, complacent, exhausted, confused, baffled, burned-out, lost, weary, depressed, disoriented, helpless, disconnected, grieving, trapped, serious, lonely, isolated, sad, gloomy, moody, somber, desperate, vulnerable, disappointed, hurt, unloved, frail, abandoned, tired, apathetic, frustrated, and bored.

Yes, there are quite a few feelings associated with this emotion. The word "disheartened" means that your heart is not whole; it is apart or reversed from itself. So, you can understand why all these feelings are making themselves known through this emotion. To become complete and together again you must pay attention to these feelings and learn from them, allow them to guide you back to your heart.

Another emotion that is often present during grief is the emotion of shame. The feelings associated with this emotion are the following:[4] humiliated, embarrassed, regretful, ashamed, sorrowful, uncomfortable, guilty, aloof, remorseful, and detached. Since emotions and feelings are universal, let's explore the ways in which shame and guilt are exposed during grief. It is important to consider the differences between shame and guilt. The experience of shame is directly related to the self as a person. With guilt, the self is not the origin of the feeling but rather the thing that was either done or not done is the focus. Shame is a painful feeling about one self, while guilt is a painful feeling of regret or responsibility for one's actions. In grief, you could feel shame and guilt by regretting something you said or did to your loved one. Also, in grief, guilt can become a difficult emotion because many believe that they are responsible for another's life in some way.

Your belief systems dominate your emotions. These beliefs are created from your social or cultural values that have been impressed upon you throughout your life. Belief systems form religions, philosophies, customs, traditions, thoughts, feelings, behaviors, and actions. It is the structure of belief systems that allows people to practice various

4 Ibid.

customs during grief. The way people mourn and grieve will greatly depend on their belief system. For example, the mourning custom for some European cultures is to wear black clothing for a period of time while grieving.

The belief system also may determine the behaviors and roles many assume within their families and relationships. The belief in these roles and behaviors will impact your ability to see truths or untruths within every experience in life, especially with the experience of the passing of a loved one. This is especially true if you are a parent or caretaker. Your belief about these roles has allowed you to see yourself as the protector and sustainer of life. It is the belief system associated with the role that assumes the responsibility. You might believe, because of your role, you could have done more and your efforts were not good enough. You blame yourself. This makes you angry and distraught. It is easier to feel this misplaced guilt rather than the death. You are playing the blame game. This always leads to shame.

The truth is no one can know how or when a person's life will end, not even your own. At times after a loss it may seem as though God had closed your eyes and ears as to allow the events for a loved one's passing to unfold. It can feel as though you were not allowed to interfere with whatever was meant to take place. Even these feeling can leave you with thoughts of shame or guilt because you may feel like you didn't do your part in some way. When it is the time for spirit to return to its true form no one can prevent it. There is freedom in knowing the only truth within relationships is to love one another. Everything is always in the hands of God.

These are timeless truths. Nonetheless, the belief that you held a place of responsibility in another's life leads you to feel all the untruths associated with shame and guilt during grief. It is shame that becomes the emotion that destroys the self. Since healing the Self is the primary reason for exploring the healing journey, then the feelings associated with shame are the most relevant as you move forward. This emotion appears in order to force you to show up in your life. Shame can become so intense that it can remove you from taking any responsibility in life, especially your own. Shame and the feelings that are associated with it can temporarily hide you from reality. This may actually offer you some healing for a while within grief so accept these feelings as your emotional guides toward transformation. However, you will eventually have to make an appearance in your life again someday. Allow shame to show you the way back to yourself.

At this point, I would like to take some time to discuss forgiveness. Forgiveness is a vital aspect of the healing process through grief. Forgiving allows you to be open to receive the grace and mercy needed to heal and to love. Through forgiveness you discover hope. The greatest act of forgiveness was when Jesus Christ was dying on the cross and He said the words, "Forgive them Father, for they know not what they do." Forgiveness is an important part of the death process because Jesus Christ offered it at the time of His death. Through forgiveness, Jesus Christ gave mercy and hope. It was through the words "Forgive them Father" that He gave hope. And through the words "For they know not what they do," He gave mercy. Through these words at the crucifixion Jesus gave the hope to know that love is always healing and giving. Then, He gave mercy for not being aware of this compassionate spirit.

When there is a lack of understanding and not knowing truth, there is hopelessness. Grief can torment the heart and deaden the spirit by attempting to rationalize the loss of a loved one with distorted lies, which can leave a sense of hopelessness when someone dies. It can remove you from all that is true and eternal. With forgiveness you are allowed to reconcile your emotions with yourself, spirit, and God. This returns you to love; this returns you to Self; and this returns you to God, which gives you hope—hope to heal.

There are many emotions that disconnect our being from truth during grief, and forgiveness is the only way back to love. Forgiveness allows your mind to respond to an experience in a new and meaningful way. Discovering a new way of life is the most difficult aspect of healing from grief; yet, it is the most necessary.

During loss, especially traumatic loss of a loved one, the mind attempts to make sense of the death, so it starts to play the blame game. This is when many people get stuck in the emotions of guilt and shame. Many become emotionally paralyzed and unable to move through their life when these emotions exhaust their thoughts during grief. Forgiveness is the only act that can create hope for living in your changing reality. Forgiveness is your only way back to life. To forgive what has been taken and how it was taken from you gives you renewed life. It is important to remember that every emotion with grief is essential and necessary. However, when these emotions consume your life, you need to take stock of your thoughts and feelings and offer yourself the love and forgiveness that allows you to find hope on your healing journey.

In my own life, not only has grief been challenging through the death of a loved one but there have been other situations where grief has made its appearance. Grief comes and goes throughout life in so many ways. Sometimes it is difficult to recognize the many faces and stages of grief. We tend to think it only appears when someone dies. Although the grief through death is the most intense, grief is present when there is any kind of traumatic life experience. When these kinds of experiences happen to me and grief is present it requires me to dig deep inside for strength and forgiveness for others as well as toward myself. Often in life there is no one harder on you than you. Forgiveness of yourself has nothing to do with you being or acting wrong. But it has everything to do with getting right with your life and offering love to yourself through it all. Then you can move forward and embrace life again with open arms and a peaceful heart. "*Forgiving the Unforgivable*" written by Beverly Flanigan, M.S.S.W., is a book that helps to understand the importance and meaning of forgiveness. I offer you the following quotations from this book so that you can understand the process of forgiveness and its ability to move you forward right now as you are healing from grief through a death or from any other difficult life circumstance. Consider reading these quotes a few times so that your mind can gain the value of forgiveness and your heart will begin to search for the ways to offer it either to someone else or most importantly, to yourself.

> "Forgiveness is a rebirth of hope, a reorganization of thought, and a reconstruction of dreams. Once forgiving begins, dreams can be rebuilt. When forgiving is complete, meaning has been extracted from the worst of experiences and used to create a new set of moral rules and a new interpretation of life's events... Forgiving does not erase the bitter past. A healed memory is not a deleted memory. Instead, forgiving what we cannot forget creates a new way to remember. We change the memory of our past into a hope for our future."
>
> —Beverly Flanigan

There are no other words to express the importance and meaning of forgiveness than what you have just read. When you are forgiving you are healing. Forgiveness is hope.

For today, you will explore the emotions of "disheartened" and "shame. Your "To" letter will be about all your feelings, thoughts, and behaviors that are surfacing from the emotions. Write from a steady flow of thought. You will not need to edit or judge your thoughts. You are here to write as a way to purify and cleanse your being. You will ask yourself and answer the following questions: ,

- How do I feel physically and emotionally? (You can choose from the list of feelings for disheartened and shame listed for Day 8) How am I behaving or how are these emotions showing up in my life? (For example, I couldn't get out of bed, didn't feel like talking to anyone today, I was too busy to think)
- What am I telling myself through my "self talk"? (For example, I will never be happy again, no one understands me, I blame myself, I could have done more, if only I would have...)

Let your words be open and willing to express the voice of your soul. Your soul needs to rid itself of all the toxic waste that is polluting the home of its being. You do not need to judge or edit anything you write. Your purpose for this today is to carve a space out for yourself so that you can find the truth that is underneath all the emotional layers of pain and garbage. So, get out your chisel and start chipping away—you are a masterpiece waiting to be discovered. Get ready to throw out the trash!

You will begin your letter with, "To..." Once you have completed your "To" letter, take some time to be your feelings and sit quietly for a few moments. Slowly breathe in through your nose with a count of eight, and release your breath through your mouth with a count of eight. Do this three times. You are relaxed, calm, and loving. You are at ease with the moment, moving with the flow. You are healing and you are peaceful. You are now ready to move on to your "Dear" letter.

Your "Dear" letter allows words to be released from your heart so that you will know and feel truth. Wisdom and love are the jewels that exist within inner knowing of your heart and soul through spirit. Sometimes, especially during grief, these jewels become lost or tarnished, and we forget our way. Only spirit can release the parts of your soul that are no longer serving for your highest good. The "Dear" letter allows you to remember and discover your truth once again. It is when you are reunited with this innate aspect of your higher self that you will encounter valuable knowledge and gifts that will move you toward divine healing.

Let's begin your "Dear" letter. The following questions will guide you and allow you to explore your divine self in truth. These questions are designed as exploration for the soul. You will write down your answers by allowing your heart to move your hand. Learning to communicate from your heart will always lead you to a treasure chest of undiscovered riches. Your key to opening your treasure lies in your willingness and desire to explore and learn with wisdom. Exploring the depths of your soul will allow you to see spirit as truth and offer you healing from within the sacred place of your heart. This is your "spirit vision." Your spirit vision is different from your "self talk" because self talk comes from your personal sensory self, or mind, while your spirit vision comes from your God center or heart and allows you to respond with your "spirit talk".

Now, with wisdom and love as your guide from your heart center, you can message your "Dear" letter from both emotions by writing your thoughts for the following questions:

- When I listen to my heart, what is my spirit trying to express through my heart about the emotion of disheartened? and shame? (Write it out)
- What are my physical and emotional feelings when I reflect on my spirit talk for disheartened? and shame? (Write it out)
- As I reflect back on the way my heart talks to me when I am disheartened, which expressions of my spirit talk make me feel better, healthier, and whole? and shame? (Write it out)
- How can I use the emotions of disheartened and shame in ways that can better influence my life? (Keep writing!)
- Using my spirit talk, how do these new ways of thinking make me feel? (Write some more)
- Using my spirit vision, how do these new ways of thinking make me look? (For example, I can see myself peaceful, I can see myself calm) (Write it out)
- How do I behave now that I know these truths?" (Write and explore how you respond with wisdom when these emotions show up in life).

Once you have explored your heart and soul and answered these questions, you are in a place of empowerment because you have lifted the veil of deception that your emotions have allowed to cover your life. Ask yourself, "Am I willing to accept this message into my life?" Your willingness will allow truth to enter your heart.

Take some quiet time now to quietly read the inspired message your heart and soul has sent to you. Let these words from your inner being offer peace, love, and purification to your soul. You are healing. You are freeing yourself from the prison of emotional pain and grief. Consider closing the process with a silent moment of prayer to offer gratitude for your divine messages and pray your God Prayer. Your spiritual path toward healing is moving forward every day. You are making great strides in your healing process. Remember, this is not a destination, healing is a journey. Consider doing the following activity to integrate your healing process.

Activity: This activity will allow you to love and forgive yourself through all the emotional neglect that you have unconsciously inflicted upon yourself in life and especially during grief. Spend a few moments today and every day to look at your reflection in the mirror. As you see yourself, look into your eyes and say "God loves me." Let the feeling of these words move from your mind to your heart. Say this to yourself in the mirror and mean it, because it is true. Then say into your own eyes "I love you." Do this about four times, slowly and intentionally. Then, say the words "I forgive you "again, slowly and intentionally, four times. Feel the energy of these words as they anchor your heart to truth. Then close your eyes and silently repeat "I am loved; I am forgiven." When you are ready, open your eyes and see your reflection again. Place one hand on your reflection in the mirror and the other on your heart. Be thankful that this is so. And so it is.

Day 9

Another day of healing is moving you forward. You are exploring, learning, and discovering so much about yourself each day. Today, the Messaging Process will offer you insight and inspiration. Please have your pen and paper ready. Find a comfortable and quiet place to relax and to write. You will begin the Messaging Process with your affirmations, your God prayer, and your visualization/meditation. Once you have spiritually aligned yourself with these practices, you are ready to begin.

For the next two days, you will be messaging from the heart of another person just as you did on Day 5. Allow yourself to be present with this activity for today as you visit an unknown yet familiar place that exists in the universality of the heart. In the physical realm of the external everyone seems different and separate from each other. We see the physical form in various shapes, sizes, race, and ethnicities. Some are tall, short, blue eyed, brown eyed with different shades and tones of skin. There are different languages, cultures, beliefs, and customs. Most feel that since we reside in different parts of the world that we are not connected to one another. We are separated by land, oceans, mountains, and seas.

The list of ways in which we are different and separate goes on and on. But are we really so different from each other? Maybe the distance lies not in the countless miles of magnificent seas and oceans or in the physical appearances that are so obviously unique and beautiful, but the distance exists in our inability to reach. Our inability to travel beyond the natural and live above the physical renders us useless. Yet, there is a place where we are all one. It is within a universal spirit of consciousness that covers the earth and the heavens. This spirit is limitless in its ability to reach and connect. It manifests itself through physical differences so that we can discover the Spirit of One. God is waiting for you to recognize the illusion that separates and divides the one spirit of creation through its all disguises, forms, and shapes. We are all different physical forms of the same God, or Spirit, living through one heart and moving to one beat. We are the instruments of God, or love, in motion. It is God doing the reaching through you. This is the compassionate and loving Spirit of God that resides within the heart of each and every one of us. This is the unknown yet familiar place that you will visit today.

As you begin your writing today, remember that you are not different and isolated from the other grief stricken hearts that you choose to message from in this process. Your ability to become empathetic toward another as you move through your healing will allow you to engage yourself with others in a meaningful way. When your heart becomes isolated, you have excessively absorbed your own sorrow and misery into itself. You have withdrawn from life because your entire focus for existence is all about you and your pain. The only way out of this place of isolation is by moving yourself through it. You move through it by getting your mind off of yourself. This aspect of the Messaging Process allows you the opportunity to get away from yourself and briefly walk on another person's journey. As you enter into their heart you allow your heart to open. The openness will carry your thoughts away from you and release you from the captivity of your secluded heart.

Before you begin the process today, it is important to understand the differences between compassion, sympathy, and empathy. Simply stated, the language of compassion says, "things are difficult for you, you seem as though you may need help," the language of sympathy says "I am sorry for your loss," and the language of empathy says, "I feel your sadness." Empathy allows you to stand with another person in their pain and not fall. While a compassionate and sympathetic person may desire the same, it is only with empathy that the desire is fulfilled. Empathy allows you to understand the emotions of compassion and sympathy with strength and dignity. The ability to empathize depends on your ability to feel and identify your own emotions. Empathy is a self awareness skill because if you were not aware that you had experienced a certain feeling, it would be difficult for you to understand the feelings of another person. Some people experiencing grief can easily have feelings of compassion, sympathy, or empathy for another person's loss; however, some may lose touch with their own feelings and feelings for others due to a very painful grief experience or denying their grief. This activity will expand your heart by allowing you to "walk a mile in another person's shoes" and learn that when there is discomfort and pain every step is leading you back to you. There is only "one" doing the walking on the many roads that lead toward one path. The shoes may be different, but the journey the same. Let's begin your "To" letter.

Once again, you will need to consider all the other people who are experiencing the same loss as you. If one of your parents has passed, then think about the other relationships that they have had throughout their life. There are relationships with spouses, other children, siblings, parents, friends, and so on; these are the hearts you will travel through today. If you have experienced the passing a child, you will need to consider the relationships a child has had throughout their life. There are grandparents, siblings, aunts, uncles, and friends. Also consider that there are other parents who have experienced the passing of a child at the same or different ages then your child. Considering and feeling from their heart will expand your heart in some way.

Remember, this aspect of the messaging process is all about getting your mind off yourself so that you can begin to heal from the isolation of grief. Empathy allows for healing to begin because your heart will begin to allow your mind to engage in thoughts that are not only sorrowful to you but also to others. When you do this, you are growing outside of your secluded grief stricken world. You are truly healing.

So, let's continue. If you are a grandparent who has had a grandchild pass, you will do the same. Consider the relationships of your grandchild. There are the parents, sisters, brothers, aunts, and uncles. If you have lost a spouse, then you will need to consider all the relationships that a husband or wife would have had throughout their life such as their children, their siblings, their parents, their friends, and if you have experienced the passing of your husband, consider the relationships of a husband who has lost his wife.

As you can see, there are many ways to explore the universal heart. Think about the person who has passed in your life and all the other loving relationships they shared. It is through one of these relationships where you will experience the heart of loss and grief for today. Once you have made a list of relationships for consideration for today, choose a heart that your heart can explore and journey through for today's messaging activity. Let's begin with a brief example— you can explore the heart of a brother whose sister has passed by feeling his sorrow through this experience. Once your heart is attuned with his heart, you can begin your "To" letter with, "To my sister." Write all the thoughts and emotions you feel in your heart for this loss.

You may consider writing something like this:

I remember when we were young and all we had was each other. We shared so many good times together. You were always there to protect and help me. I don't know if I ever told you how much I loved you. You were my best friend. I wish we would have had more time together. I will miss you. Love, Your Brother...

Now it is your turn to write your "To" letter. You will explore more of the feelings associated with this experience. This activity allows you to get your mind off of you and think about how another person is feeling. You feel empathy for this person and express their emotions through your own similar experience with loss. You are saying, "I feel your pain because I have been here too, you are in my heart." This is a vital aspect for healing the grieving heart by opening and expanding with empathy.

Once your "To" letter is finished, take some time to be with your feelings and sit quietly for a few moments. Slowly breathe in through your nose with a count of eight and release your breath through your mouth with a count of eight. Do this three times. You are relaxed, calm, and loving. You are at ease with the moment, moving with the flow. You are healing, and you are peaceful.

You are now ready to move on to the "Dear" letter. This message will allow you to experience the oneness of spirit. For this activity with your "Dear" letter, spirit will be communicating your message through the universal heart of love. You are becoming one with the heart beat of God. —the one rhythm that is beating every heart. Through this vibration your message will be given to you. Be open and willing to receive. You must align yourself to spirit and the truth in your heart. Spirit is always loving, giving and present. Love is eternal. These truths will guide you as you write.

Let's begin with a brief example of a "Dear" letter in reference to letter from above. This letter will be messaged from the spirit of a sister to her brother. In your heart there is a place that knows the eternal words a sister would share through a message. It's the place that embraces the spirit of sisterhood. As you allow yourself to be open and willing to receive this message you are unifying your healing with the healing of all who grieve. This message is your message too. Only spirit can provide one universal truth in various forms. Your "Dear" letter may say something like this:

Dear…, our memories hold the essence of life. Every time you think of me I am there with you. Every memory lives on in the heart. It is a blueprint from spirit to remind you that I was there with you. And I will never leave you. Although you may not see me, I am still sharing moments with you, protecting you and helping you. I always knew how much you loved me and I will always know. I love you forever, Your sister…

It is now your turn to write your "Dear" letter. You will share more thoughts as you explore the heart of spirit. As you can see, this message doesn't have to come only from a sister. This is a message of truth that only the heart can send. Your "Dear" letter will offer you a similar experience as you allow the spirit to offer a healing message through your heart. Through this activity your heart and spirit are expanding beyond limits. You are growing, learning, loving, and healing every moment.

At this time, read your message from spirit quietly to yourself and consider offering a silent moment of prayer of gratitude for your divine message and the universal heart of live. Ask yourself, "Am I willing to get my mind off my own sorrow?" Your willingness will open your heart to truth. Then consider closing the process with your God Prayer. Your spiritual path toward healing is moving forward every day. You are making great strides in your healing. Consider doing the following activity to integrate your healing process.

Activity: Take yourself to one of your special places today. You can consider going to a museum, park, coffee shop, bookstore, spa, and any favorite place that really resonates with your heart. This is your special time to offer gratitude to your heart for its openness. Replenish and revitalize with an exhilarating day of fun and excitement as you treat yourself to a heartfelt and much deserved outing.

Day 10

Welcome again. Take time to align yourself spiritually with your affirmations, your God prayer, and your visualization/meditation. Be sure you are prepared to begin your writing for today. Also, find a place that is comfortable and relaxing.

Once again, you will be messaging from the heart of spirit itself. Truth is revealed through the heart. This is different from your soul, because the soul is the part of you that consists of your mind, will, and emotions. When you message from the heart of another person, you enter with your heart vision. The body, mind, and spirit connection is conceived when the truth or spirit in your heart makes contact with your soul and your soul transforms your mind with this wisdom, which allows your body to behave and respond to the healing spirit within your heart. Your heart is the chief operator of the triune connection as it transfers signals of intuitive knowledge, healing, and inspiration from eternity. The following questions will guide you as you journey. Listen to your heart as you reflect and move through the questions. The source of all spirit is in the heart, and you are invited to enter this sacred place today.

As you message for today, remember that you are expanding your heart with empathy. Through this activity you will allow yourself to experience inner emotional knowing from the heart of another person. As you receive this inner awareness, you are experiencing the similarities that exist between your heart and their heart. You are recognizing that you are not alone in your grief experience. You're heart is open and willing as you begin your journey. You can refer back to your relationship list from yesterday and choose a heart to message through for today's activity. Also, as always, you will be writing from a flow of thought so there will be no need to edit or judge your words. You will be writing on your own with five questions to guide you to the truth of spirit within your heart.

You will begin your "To" letter with the following questions: (Remember, write out your responses to each question)

- □ What would spirit express through my heart today in regard to this person's situation?
- □ What words or sentiments may have been left unsaid?
- □ What are some loving sentiments I can express through my heart for them today?
- □ What are some special memories they may have shared?
- □ What would be the most precious thought they could have of their loved one?

Once you have reflected upon and answered these questions, you can take a moment to close your eyes. Be quiet and still. Be present with all your feelings right now. Let the journey move you toward understanding, love, and empathy for yourself and others. You are peaceful and comfortable. As you begin to open your eyes, you feel refreshed and relaxed.

You are now ready to receive your "Dear" message from spirit. Your heart is open, and your soul is willing to express this inner awareness through you. You are listening from your divine inner presence that is your connection to source, the light from God within. This is your time to open up to the eternal and infinite love. Your heart vision will reveal its truth as you seek to discover your divine message. You will be guided to your truth by the *same five questions* that were used previously in your "To" letter. As you reflect upon and answer the questions, keep your heart centered on the spirit of love that is flowing to and through you as you write. Let your heart speak its truth and wisdom from eternity and know, without a doubt that you never walk alone. You will begin your message with, "Dear…"

Now that you have received your "Dear" message, you will quietly read the words to yourself and allow the love and inspiration of this moment to wash over your entire being. You are feeling loved, connected, and peaceful. You have so much gratitude that spirit has allowed you to see the truth beyond this momentary place of existence and for sharing this divine message with you. You are awake, aware, and alive. Love is eternal. Remember to ask yourself again, "Am I willing to get my mind off my own sorrow?" Your willingness will allow truth to enter your heart. Consider closing this experience with gratitude and your God prayer.

Today, you have embraced your healing journey with grace and love. You have welcomed spirit into your heart. Consider doing the following activity to integrate and honor your experience for today.

Activity: Spend time throughout your day being mindful of the ways you can reach out to others. You can start small and then move on to bigger ways as time goes on. Maybe you could hold the door for someone, let a person go ahead of you in line or in a driving lane, offer a smile to a stranger, treat a friend to coffee or dinner, call someone you haven't spoken to in a while and let them know you are thinking of them, be kind to someone who was unkind to you, volunteer your time with a organization that is meaningful to you, visit an elderly or sick person, get involved in groups that offer humane services for animals, or donate money or goods to a charity. There are so many different ways to reach out. As you move on with your healing, you may consider doing something in honor of your loved one such as organizing a walk or drive in their memory for a charity, implementing a scholarship fund in their memory, or dedicating a special work through your own passions and God given gifts. Find something that resonates with your heart, and let your heart reach another heart with love.

DAY 11

Welcome. Today you will continue to explore your feelings. You will discover a way to implement better strategies for dealing with your emotions with understanding and awareness. Allow yourself to appreciate the time you have spent doing this work and your willingness to take the journey. Once again, I am so proud of all you've done and thankful that you are back here today. Let's begin. Take time to align yourself spiritually with your affirmations, your God prayer, and your visualization/meditation. Be sure you are prepared to begin your writing for today with a pen and paper or a notebook/journal. Also, find a place that is comfortable and relaxing.

Today, you will discover that within all of these emotions there is a perfect prescription for detoxifying and purifying your life. Through the messaging process you are chipping away at the emotions that are causing you to either become stuck or lost in your life. Grief is a normal process after the loss of a loved one; however, if you find that your grief has become the way you are holding on to your loved one, then you are using grief to cover up your reality. Emotions, especially during grief, can use and abuse you if you let them.

The key to managing these emotions during grief is to understand that these emotions can take control over you but you have the power to respond with wisdom. There are opposing emotions that exist within every human being. These emotions are with you so that your soul can purify and evolve by recognizing the extreme emotions and behaviors. Your soul recognizes these behaviors when you notice another person who may be behaving extremely emotional. You might see someone become enraged in traffic and you think to yourself "what is wrong with that person, they need to control themselves." Well, the reason you notice that rage is because it exists in you. The same is true for good behaviors. You may notice that a friend is generous. Well, guess what? You are generous too. Or you may enter a room and feel the energy is inspiring, uplifting and peaceful, this is because these qualities exist in you. We all have a gamut of emotions, feelings, thoughts, and behaviors moving through us at any given moment.

Another way for your soul to recognize these behaviors is when your own emotions have beaten you down in life. You will know when you have had enough of allowing your emotional life to destroy you when you realize that things can't get any worse than this. You will say, "I have nowhere to go but up from here." At this point, your soul has spoken and you are ready to move forward. The challenge with all of this lies in becoming aware of your emotions and allowing them to guide your soul back to its truth.

As you listen to your emotional guides, you will need to know that every emotion has an opposite force. Creation manifests itself through opposing forces. For example, there are good and evil, love and hate, hot and cold, or day and night. We wouldn't know one if the other didn't exist. The tender balance of all creation lies within the harmony of all opposites. The same is true for emotions. Let's say you consider yourself to be a caring person. This is a wonderful attribute. However, within this "caring" nature exists some opposites. A caring person may find themselves having other emotions surfacing. On one hand, they might be sensitive and kind but on the other hand they might be insensitive and touchy.

The same applies with other behaviors like generosity. A generous person may find themselves dealing with some opposing emotions like feeling excessive and extravagant or greedy and cheap. While someone who may describe themselves as empathetic may find that they can feel both compassionate and loving or pitiful and aloof. Yet another example may be with an intuitive person. They may find themselves feeling connected and aware or disconnected and unaware at times. This could go on and on, but you get the point.

You never feel just one thing or another because your emotional system is fueled by degrees of intensity. You are a complex system of creation, and within you exists an internal thermostat that you can use to discern your emotions so that you can harmonize your life. Within every negative emotional thought there is an exact oppositely charged emotional positive thought. You were created to be aware of these opposing forces within you so that you can choose to operate in a way that keeps you connected to God and all life. It is vital to know that all your opposite emotions, whether they are positive or negative, always offer you the opportunity to tap into higher thoughts of yourself. These higher thoughts of yourself connect you to the nature of God and all that is harmonious in life. Your emotions are surfacing to help you find the appropriate balance, or recipe, that will guide you to use the most pure and simplest ingredients toward creating a fulfilling life.

To learn to balance your emotions with the thoughts of God provides your prescription to spiritual healing. It is here where the secret recipe is discovered. It is up to you to use your God-given prescription or recipe of emotional guidance through balance as your source to living well. When you thoughts and emotions are placed into balance they are being aligned with the loving nature of God. When you are out of emotional balance you will know because you do not feel good. You are out of alignment with God. You are in alignment with God when your thoughts and emotions are balanced and flowing in the direction of peace and love toward yourself and others. This makes you feel good because you are feeling and thinking like God. As you continue to implement the Messaging Process into your healing, you will discover the emotional intelligence that is divinely yours.

So, how does this all effect grief? For many people who are grieving, isolation is one of the emotions that many use to describe their circumstance. It is important to recognize that within this emotion are opposing forces such as being withdrawn and alone to feeling gregarious and the need to belong. These are very opposing emotions, but they are necessary in understanding the reason for the extreme sense of loneliness during grief as well as the extreme behavior of running away from the situation by keeping very busy with people and things. Both behaviors can appear in these extremes because there is a resistance to the reality of life and the death experience. Although it is very normal to feel alone during grief, it is the extreme sense of loneliness and the extreme sense of keeping busy that allow you to numb or push away the emotional affects of isolation.

It is important to feel and acknowledge your emotions during this time, because if they are numbed or pushed aside, they will only surface at another time in your life. Every emotion is healing you when you allow it to be present and move through you with awareness. Try not to resist your emotions by going to extremes. When a person comes to an understanding of their emotions, feelings, and behaviors with awareness they are able to find the balance with their emotional thermostat that can offer comfort and peace.

Here is a list of emotions that you may be experiencing at this time:

[5]stuck, abandoned, forgotten, angry, fearful, regretful, distressed, judgmental, remorseful, sad, helpless, discouraged, desolate, heartbroken, heavy, anxious, frustrated, vulnerable, offended, cheated, insecure, invisible, ignored, isolated, paralyzed, nervous, uncertain, scared, devastated, calm, serene, balanced, fulfilled, compassionate, loved, proud, receptive, warm, confident, flexible, connected, peaceful, joyful, eager, gregarious, energetic, uplifted, and light.

There are other emotions that you may feel that may not on the list, feel free to include your own emotions in the list. You can use the list of emotions to guide you as you message for today's activity.

Today, you will explore your emotional weaknesses and strengths with an understanding toward balance. You will be exploring one emotion for today, but you can always return on your own to explore further. Your "To" letter will be about all your feelings, thoughts, and behaviors that are surfacing from these emotions. Write from a steady flow of thought. You will not need to edit or judge your thoughts. You are here to write as a way to purify and cleanse your being. You will ask and answer the following questions: (Write out all your responses)

- ☐ How do I feel physically and emotionally? (Consider choosing from the list above or write your own feelings)
- ☐ How am I behaving? For example, I feel exhausted, I just want to be left alone, and I was too busy to think
- ☐ What am I telling myself through my self talk? For example, I will never feel like myself again; no one understands me; if

5 Ibid.

I keep busy this will all go away; it's good not to have time to think.

Let your words be open and willing to express the voice of your soul. Your soul needs to rid itself of all the toxic waste that is polluting the home of its being. You do not need to judge or edit anything you write. Your purpose for this today is to carve a space out for yourself so that you can find the truth that is underneath all the emotional layers of pain and garbage.

Once you have written your "To" letter, take the time to quiet yourself and close your eyes. Enter into your divine presence and be still. You are calm, safe and at ease with your heart right now. Practice your diaphragm breathing and breathe in through your nose. Let your abdomen expand to a count of eight. Then release your breath through your mouth and exhale to a count of eight. Do this slowly for three times. Open your eyes when you are ready to move on to your "Dear" letter.

Your "Dear" letter is about your spirit revealing its truth. Your "soulutions" come from the spirit within. Look at the list of emotions from above and try to discover which emotion is present with you now. Also, try to consider the opposite of the your emotion you are feeling and see if you can discern a balance, which means, if you are relating to negative emotion listed above, notice the opposite positive emotion from the list as well for your discernment. To discern means to question and recognize truth or to seek an understanding of the ways of Spirit.

As you write for today, you will use the following questions to guide your message as a tool for soul exploration. The following questions will assist you to write your message and hear the truth from spirit within. Let's begin your "Dear" letter by exploring and writing answers to each question:

- ☐ What are positive ways for me to express my truth through my "spirit talk"? For example, if I said in my "To" letter that no one

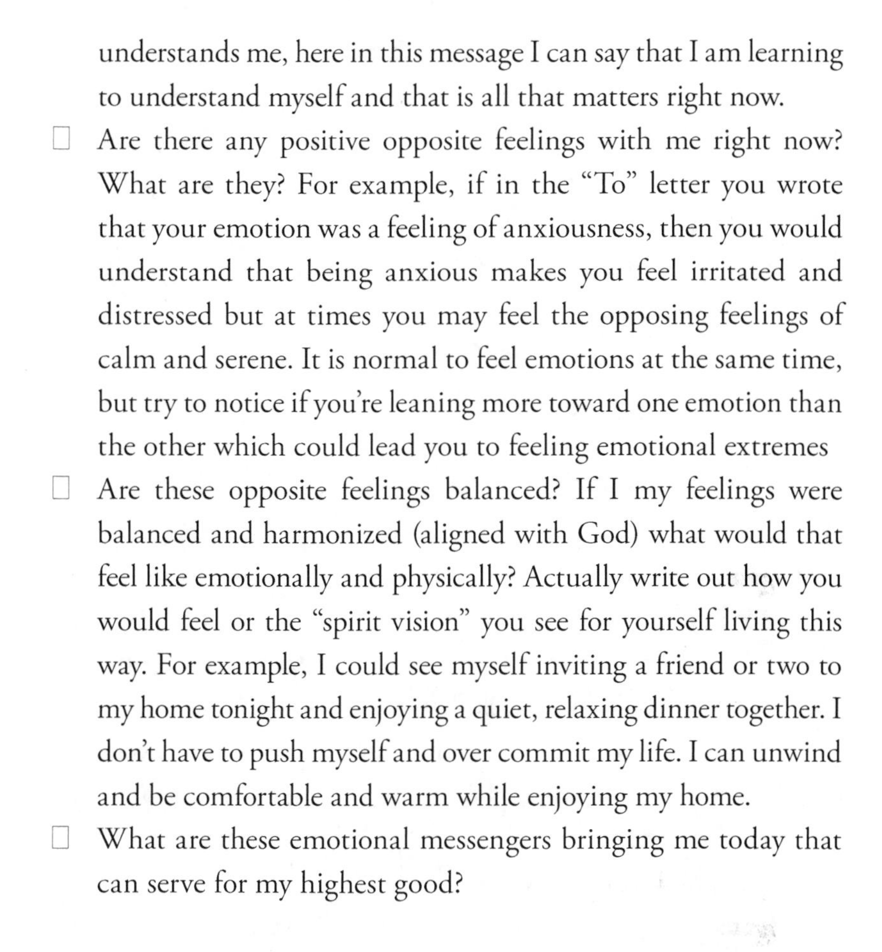

understands me, here in this message I can say that I am learning to understand myself and that is all that matters right now.

- ☐ Are there any positive opposite feelings with me right now? What are they? For example, if in the "To" letter you wrote that your emotion was a feeling of anxiousness, then you would understand that being anxious makes you feel irritated and distressed but at times you may feel the opposing feelings of calm and serene. It is normal to feel emotions at the same time, but try to notice if you're leaning more toward one emotion than the other which could lead you to feeling emotional extremes
- ☐ Are these opposite feelings balanced? If I my feelings were balanced and harmonized (aligned with God) what would that feel like emotionally and physically? Actually write out how you would feel or the "spirit vision" you see for yourself living this way. For example, I could see myself inviting a friend or two to my home tonight and enjoying a quiet, relaxing dinner together. I don't have to push myself and over commit my life. I can unwind and be comfortable and warm while enjoying my home.
- ☐ What are these emotional messengers bringing me today that can serve for my highest good?

Answer these questions truthfully and openly. Allow yourself to feel the nature of balance permeating your body, mind, and spirit.

Once you have written your "Dear" letter and received its message, you will quietly read the loving message your inner being desires to express to your soul today. Let these words cleanse and heal you. You are purifying and detoxifying your being. Consider closing the process with a silent moment of prayer to offer gratitude for your divine messages. Ask yourself, "Am I willing to accept this message into my life?" Your willingness will open you heart to truth. Close the process with gratitude and your God Prayer.

Your spiritual path toward healing is moving forward every day. You are making great strides in your healing process. Remember, this is not a destination; healing is a journey. However, please consider consulting a qualified therapist or counselor if you have persistent feelings of grief and sadness because they can better meet your needs as you move through your healing. This is only a tool or process. You can easily use this to accompany you if you seek professional guidance and support. Please consider doing the following activity to integrate your healing process.

Activity: Take a metaphysical shower. This means that while you are showering you are very aware and washing away all negativity with every motion. At first, you will pay close attention to the water temperature. Since you do this every day without thinking about it, today or tomorrow you will give the water temperature some careful thought. The reason for this is because you are understanding the importance of balance in your life. If for instance, the water temperature is too cold, you will have a very uncomfortable and quick shower experience. Your body will react with shivers and you will be anxious to get out. On the other hand, if the water is too hot, then you will be just as uncomfortable and the extreme heat will force you to leave the shower since it can hurt you and cause physical harm to your body. So you will have to think like Goldilocks and find the balance that will allow you to have a pleasurable shower experience. Once you find that perfect water temperature, your body, mind, and spirit are instantly soothed, relaxed, and calm. Now you can enjoy your shower. It is the same balance that is needed for a healthy life experience day to day.

The next part of a metaphysical shower allows you to shower with intentionality. This means that as you wash you intentionally think and say, "I wash away all negative energy; I am cleansed and purified with this healing water." As you do this, feel the power of those words and the strong stream of the water washing over your inner and outer being. As you enter into the world today, let this intention for renewing positive energy be with you throughout the day. Once you have finished your metaphysical shower, you can face your day renewed and revived. You are excited to know the harmony and balance of a new day.

Day 12

Here we are, together again, for another day of miracles as the healing process leads you to discover the eternal presence of spirit that abides in your soul. Please take time to align yourself spiritually with your affirmations, your God prayer, and your visualization/meditation. Be sure you are prepared to begin your writing for today with a pen and paper or a notebook/journal. Also, find a place that is comfortable and relaxing.

Today, you will continue to explore your emotions with an understanding toward balance and your attention on integrity. Integrity can be defined as a quality or state of being complete and undivided. Integrity allows you to be consistently aligned with your goals and values. It allows you the ability to manage and focus your objectives in life. Integrity serves as a measure of accountability. It provides you with the willingness to adjust, maintain, improve, and be consistent with life and all its outcomes. We all show up on this earth with a unique set of abilities. Since we are all different expressions of God, one persons' abilities, talents, and gifts are always different than the other. However, we all have a responsibility to magnify the beauty of God within us by properly engaging these gifts for their highest good. So it is necessary to balance your abilities with integrity.

For instance, abilities can manifest themselves through virtues or talents. That is to say, some people may be gifted with a virtue, such as confidence, while another may be gifted with talent such as singing. However, if the gifted singer lacks confidence, then their gift will not shine for the purpose that God intended for the gift. The same is true for the person with the virtuous gift of confidence. If this confident person attempted to sing and was not gifted to sing but through their confidence did so anyway, then their virtue can misguide them in their life. Recently, the world has seen "humorous" examples of this on television talent programs that are basically providing a inflated visual of what it looks and sounds like to be out of balance when your gifts and abilities do not operate with integrity. We have seen people with strong confidence that cannot carry a note to others with weak confidence whose gift to sing can carry their strength. Obviously, these are sensational extremes, yet both of these examples illustrate the imbalances within the human nature when there is an attempt to discover and serve by using your gifts with a lack of integrity. When you balance your abilities with integrity you are able to adjust, maintain, or improve your gifts, talents, and abilities so that you will be walking your divine path in life. Integrity is the corrective lens for the soul, so you can clearly envision your life's purpose.

So, how does integrity play a role in grief? The same experience that was played out above may occur in grief. A person may have a virtue of compassion, and then through misguided grief, the virtue of compassion turns into pity. Some may say that having pity is a tender hearted way of expressing mercy or sympathy, but when you turn pity toward yourself you are adjusting your love and compassion inward and you begin to feel your life as pathetic, meaningless, and powerless. These feelings do not allow you to improve your life and all its outcomes with balance and integrity. A pitiful person loses his or her power on their divine path in life. Integrity requires that you be responsible for yourself and your place in this universe. Often, grief gets you stuck in a confused perception of self and reality, therefore, your natural ways of moving through your life have shifted. Integrity is the quality within you that will allow you to navigate yourself out of these stuck and confused perceptions of grief so that you can move forward with your life with the inner guidance of divine healing. The shift that your life has experienced through the loss will be adjusted, improved and maintained with integrity.

Many people who experience loss, especially tragic loss, often exhibit fears. One of the ways fear may present itself is with your own thoughts about death. You may become afraid to die or you may want to die to be with your loved one. The fear of death and the fear to live may surface because you are feeling incomplete and separate from yourself, your loved one, and God. Through grief and loss you have lost yourself. Fear is described as the opposite of faith and a separation from love. These thoughts are allowing you to remove yourself from the fear you are facing in the present moment, which is the reality of death. So your mind chooses to separate from the reality by inputting another isolating thought, which is based on fear, so that you can continue to remove yourself from this heart breaking experience.

The farther and farther you move from your reality, the more you invite isolation and fear into your life. This will never bring you healing. Fear is torment for the soul. When you separate from love and spirit, you are not able to live in peace with the present moment. Without integrity, your mind allows fearful thoughts such as these to enter and destroy any aspect of truth. This painful isolation from truth becomes a living hell. You begin to live your life with resentment, worry, anger, shame, guilt, judgment, frustration, and so much more. You feel hopeless.

These emotions remove you from being whole and complete because you become "a house divided against itself," and a house divided against itself cannot stand because it is out of balance and removed from integrity. Integrity allows for the spirit of fear to be lifted from your soul. It allows you to know that any form of fear that is showing up in your life is only there to return you back to love. It provides for a response to grief that says, "I remember who I am, and I know my life has value and worth." Integrity makes you answer the call to life and spirit in this present moment with a knowing that you are an integral part of this place and all of eternity. You become an accountable being when you know that your emotions are your guides and you do not serve them but they serve you so that you can maintain consistency throughout your life.

Here is a list of a range of emotions with an emphasis on integrity:

[6]Conflicted, unfairness, dishonesty, diversity, disunity, abandoned, forgotten, angry, fearful, regretful, distressed, judgmental, remorseful, sad, helpless, discouraged, desolate, heartbroken, heavy, anxious, frustrated, vulnerable, offended, cheated, insecure, invisible, ignored, isolated, paralyzed, nervous, stuck, uncertain, scared, devastated, calm, serene, balanced, fulfilled, compassionate, loved, proud, receptive, warm, confident, flexible, harmonious, connected, peaceful, joyful, eager, gregarious, energetic, uplifted, light, unified, understanding, truthful, honest, complete, undivided, honorable, sincere, and sound.

Once again, it is normal to experience any of these emotions during grief. However, if you are finding yourself having extreme emotional experiences then you are allowing your emotions to dominate your life. Extreme emotional behavior refers to an emotion that seems to be more present for a period of time. Don't let the word "extreme" alarm you, the reason for the use of this word is only to signal you to become aware of your emotional tendencies so that you can create a space to align your emotions.

The only way you will know if your emotional strengths or weaknesses are tending to move your life forward with balance and integrity is by becoming aware. Allow yourself to pay attention to how and when these emotions show themselves to you throughout the day. Think of them as guests who are popping in to provide you with some essential information about yourself. If "disunity" has shown up it will probably display itself as conflict, resentment, cheated, unfairness, or anger just to name a few emotions. Its appearance will manifest through your behavior; for example, you might find yourself arguing with people more frequently, having difficulty sharing with your finances, time, and energy or you may feel a sense of "victim" superiority over another person by thinking your circumstances are worse than theirs.

---

6 Ibid.

Some may have thoughts or acts of vengeance toward another if a death was a result of an intentional act. This kind of experience with death is very difficult for many. It helps to remember that God is all ruling (Almighty). Through spirit, God is everywhere and knows all things. It is integrity that allows you to remember this truth in God as the knower of all beings, of all creation, and of divine justice. Integrity allows you to understand that any kind of negative action taken will not right a wrong. It allows you to "let go and let God" for it is God's justice that is greater than any force of human capabilities. In Romans 12:17–21 it says, "Do not repay anyone evil for evil. Be careful to do what is right in the eyes of everybody. If it is possible, as far as it depends on you, live at peace with everyone. Do not take revenge, my friends, but leave room for God's wrath, for it is written: 'It is mine to avenge; I will repay', says the Lord. On the contrary, if your enemy is hungry, feed him; if he is thirsty, give him something to drink. In doing this you will heap burning coals on his head. Do not be overcome by evil, but overcome evil with good."

Still, many may be find this can difficult to live by, but with integrity at your side, you can try to think of the behaviors that surface in your day-to-day life to see if your emotions are being balanced and managed. You learn to balance your emotions with integrity by being aware and willing to align yourself with the wholeness of your nature and the consciousness of all that is natural. This means you make a conscious decision to become accountable for your behaviors and emotions in a more balanced way so that you become released from the unconscious tendencies that have caused you to shift your perception of self and reality. It means you are discovering your complete and true nature. A willingness to operate with integrity allows you to balance your life and realize your connection to each other as you choose to respond with harmony and unity to all your circumstances.

Today, will be much like yesterday as you begin your Messaging Process. You will explore your emotional weaknesses and strengths with an understanding toward balance and integrity. You will explore one emotion for today, but you can always return on your own to explore further. Your "To" letter will be about all your feelings, thoughts, and behaviors that are surfacing from these emotions. Write from a steady flow of thought. You will not need to edit your thoughts. You are here to write as a way to purify and cleanse your being.

You will ask and write out the answers to the following questions:

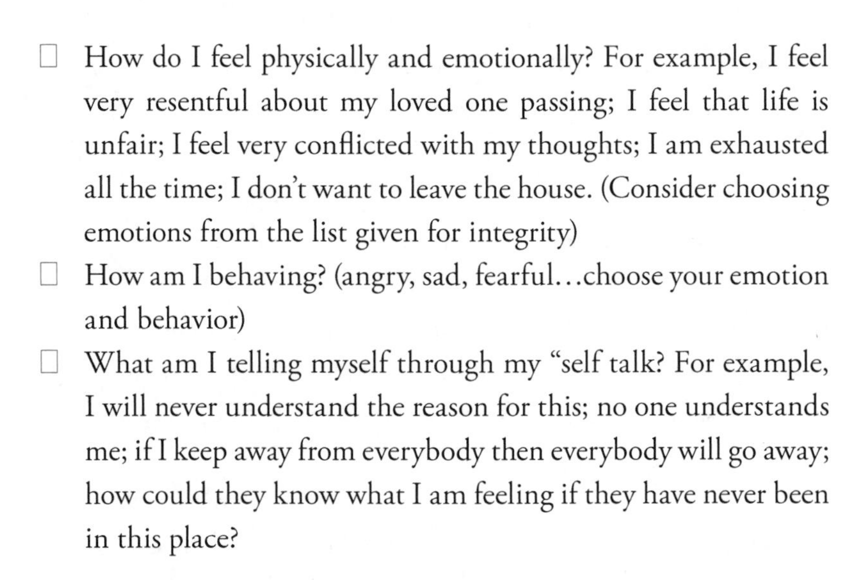

- ☐ How do I feel physically and emotionally? For example, I feel very resentful about my loved one passing; I feel that life is unfair; I feel very conflicted with my thoughts; I am exhausted all the time; I don't want to leave the house. (Consider choosing emotions from the list given for integrity)
- ☐ How am I behaving? (angry, sad, fearful…choose your emotion and behavior)
- ☐ What am I telling myself through my "self talk? For example, I will never understand the reason for this; no one understands me; if I keep away from everybody then everybody will go away; how could they know what I am feeling if they have never been in this place?

Let your words be open and willing to express the voice of your soul. Your purpose for this today is to create a space for yourself so that you can find the truth that is underneath all the emotional turmoil that has crept in and blurred your focus in life.

Once you have written your "To" letter, take the time to quiet yourself and close your eyes. Enter into your divine presence and be still. You are calm, safe, and at ease with your heart right now. Practice your breathing and breathe in through your nose let your abdomen expand to a count of eight. Then release your breath through your mouth and exhale to a count of eight. Do this slowly for three times. You are open, whole, and complete. You are moving forward with balance and harmony. Open your eyes when you are ready.

You are now ready to move on to your "Dear" letter. Your "Dear" letter is about your soul revealing its truth: your "soulutions" through spirit. Look at the list of emotions from above and try to discover which emotion is present with you now. Also, try to consider the opposite of all your emotions you are feeling and see if you can discern a balance. As you write for today, you will use the following questions to guide your message as a tool for soul exploration. The following questions will assist you to write your message and hear the truth from spirit within.

Let's begin your "Dear" letter by exploring and answering each question: (Write out all your responses)

- What positive feelings of integrity are with me right now? For example, if in the "To" letter you wrote that you were feeling like life is unfair then you would understand that other emotions exist with unfairness from feelings of injustice and wronged to righteous and equality. A range of emotion such as this can be acted out with negative physical and emotional behaviors or with positive actions of charity and benevolence toward others. It is normal to feel opposing emotions at the same time, but try to notice if you're leaning more toward one emotion than the other which could lead you to feeling emotional extremes and pay attention to how these emotions are showing up for you in life and meet them with positive words of integrity from the list above.
- What are positive ways for me to express my truth through my "spirit talk"? For example, if I said in my "To" letter that I will never understand the reason for this loss then you can express here that there can possibly be a greater reason that I am just not aware of right now or ready to understand at this point in my life, or maybe my broken heart can be pieced back together by the spirit within me, or I am finally seeing that the heart is where my home is and nothing can be lost in this sacred place (write the message that your heart is sending through you).

- ☐ If my feelings were balanced and harmonized with integrity (aligned with God), what would that feel like emotionally and physically? Use positive emotions from the list on integrity to guide you with this response and actually write out how you would feel or the "spirit vision" you see for yourself living this way. For example, you might write a message that says, I could see myself living with understanding toward my friends and family. I am living connected to with others. I am not judging my life and circumstances or anyone else's. I see myself being peaceful with my life and sharing this new way of being with others. Today, I will have understanding for myself, and I will love myself through this so that my presence will be uplifting to another person who has experienced a loss or hurt in their life too.
- ☐ And finally, what are these emotional messengers bringing me today that can serve for my highest good and wholeness?

Answer these questions truthfully and openly. Allow yourself to feel the nature of balance and integrity permeating your body, mind and spirit.

Once you have written your "Dear" letter and received its message quietly, read your divine message to yourself and allow the healing presence of each word to purify and cleanse your soul with infinite love. Remember to ask yourself, "Am I willing to accept this message in to my life?" Your willingness will open your heart to truth. You can consider closing the process with a silent moment of prayer to offer gratitude for your divine messages. Close the process with your God Prayer.

Your spiritual path toward healing is moving forward every day. Remember, this is not a destination, healing is a journey. It is a journey of discovery. There may be days when you feel better or worse than other days, no matter the kind of day you are having, every day is an opportunity to use your emotional awareness and meet your emotions with integrity, balance, wisdom, and love. The power to respond to your emotions lies within you. These are the times in your journey when you can be mindful of your discoveries so that the obstacles in your path can be stepping stones not stumbling blocks. But please keep in mind once again considering consulting a qualified therapist or counselor if you have persistent feelings of grief and sadness since they can better meet your needs as you move through your healing. This is only a tool or process. You can easily use this to accompany you if you seek professional guidance and support. God is in all forms of healing. Trust your inner guidance to seek out ways to offer healing to your heart. Please consider doing the following activity to integrate your healing process.

Activity: Take a moment before you fall asleep tonight to release all negative thoughts and emotions to the light and the presence of God. Ask and allow for the light of God to be present while you sleep and replenish your consciousness with guidance, love, peace, and the complete wholeness of all that is divine. Always end your day with gratitude to God for eternal love and constant goodness. Also, in this moment ask for spirit to reveal in your dreams a beautiful truth about your life and its circumstances. Although it may be difficult right now, try to focus your thoughts on love and gratitude about something good from your day each night before you fall asleep. Have a peaceful night's rest and sleep well in the silent wisdom of the divine.

Day 13

Welcome to this new day to walk the healing path together. Your journey is moving forward with great success. Allow yourself to appreciate the time you have spent doing this work. I am so proud of all you've done and thankful that you are back here today. You should be very proud of your strength and commitment to this process too. Let's begin. Take time to align yourself spiritually with your affirmations, your God prayer, and your visualization/meditation. Be sure you are prepared to begin your writing for today with a pen and paper or a notebook/journal. Also, find a place that is comfortable and relaxing.

Today, you will journey to a place within your heart that feels empty, lost, and broken. It is a place that sheltered an important part of you. This vital aspect of your being is called the Self. The Self is the whole and complete aspect of your being, different for the self, which is your personality. It is during times of loss when a person can lose touch with the Self.

Every relationship, especially the closest relationships, serves as a way for us to experience ourselves. Therefore, when you experience the passing of someone very loved and dear to you, you are not only experiencing the loss of your loved one but you are also experiencing a loss of you. This person allowed you to see a part of you through their existence that you would have never known existed in you if they had not been a part of your life. You experience your true Self through the people and relationships that surround you in your life.

During grief, it is normal to feel as though a piece of you is missing because you are not only missing your loved one but you are also missing yourself as well. You are missing the way the relationship expressed you and the Self that you came to know and live through. The language of grief often communicates this very clearly with sayings like, "I feel like a part of me is missing," "I died the day they died, my heart is broken.", These expressions go on and on when a loved one passes because your heart is attempting to reconcile to the Self. Your heart is searching for you, looking to find that part of you that is lost and seeking its way home again.

The only way home to yourself again is to find the eternal essence of you that is spirit. Your loved one has returned to their place of wholeness and completeness through eternal spirit. It is now your turn to do the same. Death is a passage to a new way of being, a new life, or resurrection. When a loved one passes, it is not only their form that has shifted but yours has too. The Self in you is learning, growing, and evolving through this experience. Once again, you are seeing your true Self through this relationship, even if you think it has ended physically, you are still experiencing through it because spirit never dies. The passing of your loved one is another way that this relationship allows you to experience your true Self. Through death, you discover your higher being because you are losing your attachment to the physical and gaining spirit. You are becoming more Self aware and spiritually awake. Allow the Self to navigate a path back to your heart during this time of grief and find its way home again.

Today, you will be messaging to and from your Self. As you begin the process today, think about all the dialogue you have with yourself and what this "talk" is really trying to express through you. Our words are very powerful, and each word shows up to convey meaning about our emotions, circumstances, and personality. Think about the words and phrases you have been expressing through your grief experience and learn from them. As you begin your "To" letter for today, let the words flow from a steady stream of thought. You will not need to edit or judge your thoughts. You are here to write as a way to purify and cleanse your being.

You will ask and write out the answers to the following questions:

- What would I express to Self today in regard to my situation?
- What words or sentiments are surfacing right now in regard to myself?

Let your words be open and willing to express the Self within. Your "To" letter may say something like this:

To Self, living with the loss of my loved one has been one of the most difficult experiences of my life. I don't feel like I am the same person and I don't think I will ever be that person again. A part of me just isn't here anymore. From, …

Your message will be more expressive as you journey to your heart and pick up the pieces of your Self that grief has left broken and lost inside of you. You are here today to mend and recover the part of you that wants so much to be found and brought back home again. As you write, recognize the language of grief as your way of sensing the territory of a lost heart. Let the words search your heart and provide clues to the essence of your true nature. Your higher being is waiting to be found and love you back from this desolate and barren space of separation. You are reuniting with the being of your nature as you message for today. Once you have reflected upon and answered these questions, you can take a moment to close your eyes. Be quiet and still. Be present with all your feelings right now. Let the journey move you toward Self. You are peaceful and comfortable. As you begin to open your eyes, you feel refreshed and relaxed.

You are now ready to receive your "Dear" message from Self. Your heart is open and willing to express this inner awareness through you. You will be guided to your truth as you message from Self today. Let your heart be centered on the spirit of love that is flowing to and through you as you write. You will begin your message with writing your responses to the following questions:

- What would be the most precious thoughts, words, or sentiments my loved one could have of me?
- What are the most precious thoughts, words, or sentiments Self could have of me?
- How is this experience allowing me to remember and journey back to my true Self?

You will message to these questions on your own without a sample for guidance because your Higher Self intuitively knows the way that is best for you to respond. Allow the words to lead you back to a familiar place as you enter your higher consciousness to a loving presence. You are now ready to begin your message with "Dear Self…". Once you have written your message, take a silent moment to read your divine message from Self and listen to the words with love and appreciation; for this is how they were given to you. Your divine message from your Self awareness has revealed its truth to you. Let this message purify your being. At this time, consider offering a silent moment of prayer of gratitude for your divine messages. Then consider closing the process with gratitude and your God Prayer. Your spiritual path toward healing is moving forward every day. You are making great strides in your healing. Consider doing the following activity to integrate your healing process.

Activity: This activity will allow you to explore your interests, gifts, and passions in life. You are going to make a list by dividing a sheet of paper into three columns. In the first column you will label My Interests, the second column is labeled My Gifts, and the last column is labeled My Passions. In each column, brainstorm as many things as you can think of about yourself. You may notice that you are writing the same things in each column. That is fine because many times all these aspects all related. For instance, you may be interested in photography, and you may have been told that you have a gift in this area, so it may be very possible that you have a passion for photography.

As you make your lists, think about the things you would love to try or learn that may not be typical for you, but somewhere inside you know that you have a desire to explore. It may be acting, belly dancing, exercise, running, walking or hiking, swimming, Tai Chi, traveling, horseback riding, meditating, painting, singing, writing,or sewing—anything that is in your heart waiting to be expressed, anything that excites you, anything creative, include it on your lists. Then, draw a picture of yourself doing this desired activity. Be imaginative, and as you draw really feel a sense of yourself as being healed and enjoying life. See it in your mind and draw the image as beautifully as you can onto the paper. Have fun with this activity. Explore your desires, passions and gifts. Once you have made your lists and completed your drawing, take a moment to notice all the wonderful and diverse aspects of your being. Appreciate and acknowledge your beauty. See the joy and awe that is magnificently you!

Day 14

Your healing journey is moving forward as the Messaging Process nears its final day. You have been working with diligence and fortitude each and every day. You should be proud and grateful of all the work and progress that you have made. I am so grateful to have spent these days with you as you have allowed for this process to become a part of your life. You will continue your Messaging Process today with your thoughts toward God. Let's begin by taking time to align yourself spiritually with your affirmations, your God prayer, and your visualization/meditation. Be sure you are prepared to begin your writing for today with a pen and paper or a notebook/journal. Also, find a place that is comfortable and relaxing.

Yesterday, you journeyed to the Self as you searched your heart for the missing part of you that the death experience may displace from your being, and you discovered your true nature. At times, the passing of a loved not only detaches you from Self but it also separates you from God. Through relationships with loved ones and others in our lives we come to know ourselves, but more importantly we come to know God. You and everyone you will ever know or meet in life in an expression of God's spirit. Our relationships are an exchange of energies that include the physical, mental, emotional, psychological, and spiritual. Death creates a shift in the flow these energies. Healing allows for a balance to be restored. To return to your true Self, nature or spirit is to find your way back to the God within, Source, or Love. You are journeying to God as you are healing. On this journey it is important to wear the garments that have been designed for you. Remember to put on love, hope, faith, kindness, gentleness, patience, mercy, tenderness, good temper, and forgiveness for others and for yourself.

These are the essentials for every heart traveling the healing journey. And these are the essentials that you grieve or miss when a loved one passes. All of these essentials are expressions of God that you see manifested in your most beautiful relationships and within your true nature. But somehow death removes the ways of God and withdraws your ability to see the beauty that is always present. It is this disconnect from God that causes a dejected spirit. The healing process allows you to encounter the ever-present, loving spirit of God that is the ultimate presence within yourself. The oneness of God within the Self is the infinite reality of eternal love and wholeness.

Love is the only aspect of you that is real. This is why it hurts so much when love feels like it's gone forever. This feeling makes you lose touch with your reality, your truest Self, and God. The love we give to each other always ascends to One Spirit, to God. Therefore, love can never be lost because it is ultimately for God even though we are expressing it toward another.

Healing during grief allows for you to discover your way of being that exists beyond your physical nature and self perception. This is your ultimate reality. To discover your ultimate reality is one of the greatest gifts of grief. It binds you with all that is spirit and eternal. Once again, it is important to know that is normal to feel disconnected and sorrow during grief since human nature reacts to painful circumstances, but it is the spiritual nature that allows for the light to shine through the darkness to guide you toward peace and healing.

The language of losing touch with God during grief often sounds like this: "why would God allow for something like this to happen? where was God when this happened? where is God's love now? where were you God when I needed you? God, why couldn't you save them?" The questions of a lost heart go on and on. This language is very familiar for many of us who grieve. These questions are here during grief because your heart is searching for God. The questions form when you feel that God is a being outside of you that can make good or bad things happen. Through this experience you learn to doubt and not trust God. Then, you doubt and not trust yourself or others. You become separate from God, yourself and others. Yes, we must know that God is everywhere but when it comes to healing it is vital to remember the power of God is always working within you now and always.

Through the language of grief you can see that you are losing touch with God. Yet there is a realization that these words are driving you back to you and the God within you. This language is you questioning your Higher Self as you search for the divinity within. You are realizing that this death experience is allowing you to remember God and the spirit of love that is eternal. Although the language is expressing as doubt and anger, you are really questioning love and searching for faith. You are asking if you love me why make me hurt this bad. Without God's love present in your heart you are disconnecting with all that is hope, all that is love and all that is faith. You have disconnected from all that is you.

Since love is your only true reality, your reality has been shaken and morphed through the death experience. Yet it is only through asking these questions and expressing the language of grief in this way that you will attempt to reconnect to love, and to God. Through hope (**HOPE** is **H**aving **O**nly **P**eace **E**veryday or **H**aving **O**nly **P**ositive **E**nergy), faith, and love you can attempt to believe in your reality again, to believe in yourself and the God within. It is in the unity of love and spirit that God manifests as the ultimate knower of your being.

God's spirit is infinite. The same spirit that is with you is with everyone and in everything. This includes human being, animal and mineral. All experiences express God. It is the human intellect that defines them as good, bad, tragic, and so on. The God Spirit within only knows your ultimate and infinite truth and reality, and it will allow every experience, whether you may think they are good or bad, to manifest in order for your being to remember and know its divine nature.

In the Book of Genesis, God tells Eve not to eat from the tree in the midst of the garden. This is the tree of good and evil. Eve believed that eating the fruit from this tree could give her knowledge, and that she would know all that was good and all that was evil. Just like Eve, we cannot know what is truly good or evil, because we are searching for the answer outside of ourselves. When you look around at your circumstances in your life you perpetuate the experience. It is tempting for the human mind to do this, because it seems simpler and more obvious to find knowledge outside yourself.

It is through your union with God where you discover the wisdom and strength to move through your circumstances. To seek union with God allows you to tend to the inner garden, not the outer garden. Paradise is found, not lost. Since we are made in the image and likeness of God, we have the presence and nature of God within us, which is true life within us. Therefore, we are given the gift of life and free will as we live. It is the intuitive sensing of God that gives guidance to the mortal-conscious mind in every moment of life. Through God's presence within us we know how to behave "good" and not "bad" toward ourselves and each other. However, when wrong things happen to us or others in life; it is not within our natural human sensibilities to know if this was actually the best or worst circumstance for us or others. Only God, the knower of our being, knows the depths of our hearts and souls so that every aspect of our life can allow us to ascend to the fullest union with God. When there is an attempt to attain the knowledge of what is good or bad for ourselves or others in life it will deceive you and separate you from God.

To try to rationalize the ways of God when it comes to suffering, death, or pain in life can only move us further and further away from God. This is the human intellect that is attempting to discover the answer to life's greatest mysteries. In the mind of God the label of good and evil does not exist. This label only exists in the human intellect through our personal sense of selfhood. However, the closer you move toward the presence of God the more you will become aware to the mysteries of the divine, because God will impart sacred wisdom to your heart. You will receive revelation from God.

When you allow all of your life experiences to align with your Higher Self, Spirit, or God, you are becoming whole and one with all of eternity. However, it is true that it is difficult to align with God when there is suffering, because we think God can remove the experience from our life. Suffering separates you from the spirit of God within you and makes you feel like there is a greater power outside of you that can change things. This is deception, it is not truth. You, through the spirit of God in you, have the power to change your life. If we look at the life of Jesus, we can learn that although he was an enlightened being, which means the immortal aspect of his mortal nature was not hidden from itself, he struggled with this human aspect of self as well. The struggle with these feelings within Jesus surfaced because his being took on all the sins and suffering of humanity and so his divine nature was feeling all the pain of the sensory self just as we do.

The Gospel of Luke 22:39–44, it tells of Jesus going to the Garden of Gethsemane where he prayed, "Father, if you are willing, take this cup from me; yet not my will but your will be done." Jesus prayed with such anguish that it says, "His sweat was like drops of blood falling to the ground." Jesus saw all the suffering of mankind, and he knew the suffering and torture that was ahead of him. His soul was tormented by fear, anxiety and negative emotions. And so, he asked to let this pass from him but only if it be the will of God. Yet, Jesus knew that the will of God was his will in truth. Jesus also knew that this experience was the reason and purpose for his soul to incarnate. For this reason he knew that it all had to take place as it did. The human aspect of his nature was deeply overwhelmed with sorrow, yet his divine nature saw the plan through to the finish.

The same is true for us. Our souls have a purpose, and every experience allows our souls to live out their missions for existing in this world. It is the divine power within you that brings you into union with God, even when you're suffering. However, to be in complete union with the perfect will of God (which is your will in truth) requires absolute obedience at all times. The word obedience means to listen or hear forward. As human beings it is difficult to be in this divine union, especially during trials. But if you listen to the silent voice of God within you, then you can hear the moments of healing that are moving forward with you and you will obey. When you place all your pain and suffering into the sacred dwelling of the heart, your being will the find its divinity through the peace of God and you will be able to endure the trials as they come with trust that it all is unfolding as it should for the sake and sanctification of your soul. Then you will have union with God until God's will, which is your will in truth, is finished as well.

Ultimate unity exists in the heart of all that is one with God. It is where eternal love and spirit reside. This is the healing power of God working in you and welcoming you home. Spirit always searches for home, and home is where the treasures of your heart are secure and safe. Many say that God is love. This saying is true, because love is a creative energy that activates your feelings. Love is action, it is motion. Love is the energy of God moving in you. It is the spiritual energy that transforms your soul. More importantly, in the natural sense of the word, love is a decision. Your feelings tell you whether or not you should love. The emotional aspect of our being overrides the energy of love because the conscious mind is led by it thoughts and feelings. This is especially true during life challenges such as grief. It is your reaction to those conscious thoughts and feelings that create a behavior. This is free will. Free will is your decision to either follow your emotions or physical nature or align yourself with truth which is your spiritual nature. God does not force you to love but love forces you to God. It is this spiritual force that never dies or departs from us.

While you are making these considerations about love, God waits for your return with eternal love toward you. Your response to your feelings will demonstrate your choice, or free will, which always leads to God's will or your will in truth. If you feel like there is emptiness in your heart, then consider asking with all you have remaining inside of you for God and Spirit to come into your heart. You could say, "God, come into my heart. Spirit come into my heart., I am one with God and Spirit," or "Jesus, come into my heart. You are my Lord and Savior." Your own personal experience with faith and spirituality will allow you to open the door to the sacred dwelling of the heart to discover the love has never left you.

In your heart you will encounter infinite love, eternal spirit and God. It is God's greatest desire for you to heal. God dwells within you as a seed, but only through your choice to love can you cultivate the seed and let it bloom as your strength, your peace, the lover of your spirit, the dreamer of your heart, the knower of your being, and the healer of your soul.

The powerful presence of God is within you as you journey—that's the good news. Let this divine power comfort and heal you from this place of grief. Your healing journey is allowing you to remember your sacred inner life. You are becoming one with all that is spirit though your healing experience. Your relationship to the God within will allow you to return to yourself again, because you are returning to love. And where there is love, there is peace. You will find the lost you that you are searching for in the midst of grief. A new life and way of being awaits you on this journey. This is the you that your soul has been yearning to know. Every step is mapping your way toward the treasures of your heart, the essence of spirit, the discovery of Self, and your union to God. With the love of God, Self, and the love and spirit of your loved one as the keys to the treasures of your heart, you will allow all the secret riches of heaven to open and pour blessings to and through your being as you discover your truth on this journey. Always keep them with you as you travel through grief, for each holds your well-being and power for healing.

Today, you will be messaging to and from God. Let your words and thoughts be open and willing to express all your thoughts and feelings. You are here today eliminating all the toxic feelings that have been poisoning your soul. Allow these feelings to be released from you as you begin to find your way back to love, spirit, and God. These words will be your stepping stones that lead you toward wholeness and oneness with God. To be whole means to not live in negativity or at lower levels of consciousness. To be whole means to function from your higher self or the God within. Your words in this message will empty all you of all your negativity and guide you to a place inner unity.

As you begin your "To" letter for today, let the words flow from a steady stream of thought. You will not need to edit or judge your thoughts. You are here to write as a way to purify and cleanse your being. You will ask and write out your answers to the following questions:

- What would I express to God today in regard to my situation?
- What would I like to tell God about grief and loss and how it has affected my life?
- What words or sentiments are surfacing right now that I need to express to God?

Let your words be open and willing to express. There will not be an example here to illustrate the language and expressions of your grief with words to God, because only you know the feelings that you need to release at this point of the process. Any outside guidance can infiltrate your own flow of thought and cause you not to fully express your own message to God.

So, here you are—write all that you need to let God know about your loss. This is your chance to let it all out and say everything that has been held inside your heart and mind. You are here today to mend and recover the part of you that wants so much to be found and brought back home again. Let it all out. The God within you is waiting to hear from you.

You will begin your "To" message with, "To God…". Once you have reflected upon and answered these questions, you can take a moment to close your eyes. Be quiet and still. Be present with all your feelings right now. Let the journey move you closer to God. You are peaceful and comfortable. As you begin to open your eyes, you feel calm and relaxed.

You are now ready to receive your "Dear" message from God. You are listening from your divine inner presence that is your connection to source, the light from God within. This is your time to open up to where the eternal exists and dwells within its infinite love. You will be guided to the one and ultimate presence of God as you message for today. This is the place of your ultimate truth and reality. Allow the spirit of God to move and breathe and manifest its true nature. Let your words and life be God's expression for you to experience your divine truth. As you write from God today align your heart with the spirit of love that is flowing to and through you.

You will begin your message and write out your responses to the following soul exploration questions,

- What are some loving sentiments God could express to me in regard to my situation today?
- What would be the most precious thoughts, words, or sentiments eternity could share with me right now?
- What are the most precious thoughts, words, or sentiments God could have of me right now?
- If God could speak to me about grief and loss, what would be said right now?
- How is this experience allowing me to remember and journey back to God?"

You will message to these questions on your own without a sample for guidance, because the God within, the knower of your being, is the only source that can create the purest expressions as you message for today. Allow the words to turn your thoughts around and lead you back to a familiar place as you enter your higher consciousness to the loving presence of God.

You are now ready to begin your message with "Dear ...".Once your divine message from the inner oneness of God has revealed its truth to you, spend some to read the message to yourself and reflect and contemplate on the inner beauty, love, and unity of God within your sacred being. Let God's wisdom be absorbed into your soul. Allow God's compassionate spirit to bring love and peace to your inner being. Let the inner light of God sublimate any darkness within your soul with its pure radiance so that the awesome power of God can be magnified through your life.

Consider offering a silent moment of prayer and gratitude for your inspired and loving message from God. Then, consider closing the process with gratitude and your God Prayer. You are whole and complete. Your spiritual path toward healing is a journey you will continually travel day to day. There is no final destination for your healing since every day will take you through various states of awakening as you move toward your ultimate truth, reality, and union with God. Be open, aware, and loving with the inner and outer aspects of your life and being as your path unfolds before you. Embrace life and spirit each and every moment, and know that all of eternity is with you always. Consider doing the following activity to integrate your healing process.

Activity: Look back over your lists and drawings from yesterday's activity. On these lists you have written all your interest, gifts, and passions. You have actually felt and seen yourself doing this activity in your heart and have drawn the image of yourself. Today, you will chose one interest, one gift, and one passion that you can commit and schedule to either learn or do today and in the days ahead. If one of your passions was to paint, then you will begin painting or seek out a way to learn how to paint and schedule yourself in a class. As you do or learn from these aspects of your being, you become empowered and inspired by your inner spirit or God. You will contact your divinity by knowing that as you move and do all these wonderful new and exciting activities you are allowing God to move and do through you. Once you know who walks along with you every day and as you explore new areas of yourself, you will become stronger in both your inner and outer life. As you move through your life and discover your new way of being in this world, always remember the Bible verse from Matthew 19:26 that says, "With God all things are possible."

Day 15

You've made it! Your final day of the Messaging Process has arrived. You are very a strong person, because you have allowed this process to be with you as you heal. You have worked so hard to get to this point. I know I have said it before, but today it is so important to say how grateful and proud you should be of yourself to be here right now and I am honored to have shared this experience with you. This has been a journey of exploration into the depths of your heart and soul during this very difficult time in your life. Your commitment to this process and to yourself is a true testament of your ability to move forward with your healing and to discover your hidden truth and beauty that grief has covered. Every day from here and on will be a day of recovery, restoration, and renewal as you continue on your healing path with God and Spirit.

Each day during this process you have aligned your triune being through affirmations, visualization and meditation. You will do the same today. I would like to encourage you to continue to do this every day of your life. Think of it like brushing your teeth and getting dressed for a new day each morning. Make it part of your routine. As you implement all three spiritual techniques into your daily life, you will fortify yourself with the peace, hope and love that holds and guides you at all times. These practices will allow you to be in contact and attuned to God and spirit for now and for always. I implore you to use these techniques to sustain you and keep you connected each day.

The healing journey should not be an experience of coping through your sorrow and pain. The purest kind of healing comes forth when you cooperate with spirit and allow the experience to move through you with awareness and openness. Your entire existence is of a triune nature. Just as your body, mind, and spirit require balance for optimal functioning so does your past, present, and future require balance and harmony for your well being. Your past and future all comprise this one moment right now. It is how you choose to think, act, and behave in this moment that will create your future. Also, everything that was a part of your past is here with you now and will move into the future with you. This is why is important to consider holding on to the beauty of all in life and let go of past and present happenings that do not serve for your highest good. All you have is this moment, right here and right now. Try not to look back or forward, just look within and you will discover the power of spirit and its ability to sustain you on the divine path of life.

With all of this being said, as you continue to move forward each day you may find you are taking two steps forward and three steps back on this journey. When this happens, be patient, loving, gentle, and kind to yourself. Embrace the moment, and allow it to take you to a new height of awakening. The journey of spiritual healing will bring you to your own inner road, your eternal path. This is your time to explore and notice a path that you have already traveled but you are now able to see with your acquired vision of spirit and awareness. This divine vision will allow you to soar to majestic heights as you overcome a challenging road from your past experience. It is like hiking on path that you have walked before and each time you explore this path you discover new sights of wildlife and landscapes.

Often nature will offer you its bountiful display of the changing seasons to inspire you as you walk. Yet even though you have been to this place many times before, you are always amazed and in awe of all the new discoveries that the trip brings to you. You aren't going backward when this happens to you. You have been given the opportunity to revisit your path with awareness, gratitude, and inspiration, since these are the acquired gifts from your journey. This is your time to appreciate and acknowledge your gifts. It is your time to reflect on where you have been and look with faith toward the journey ahead. When you walk through healing you may have to retrace your steps to gain your footing so that you can travel with clarity, confidence and determination. This is your opportunity to heal again with wisdom. You are traveling this inner road again for a reason— make the trip a worthy experience and continue without judgment or expectation for each bend and turn.

To release your expectations toward yourself and others as you heal allows for you to place your hope in God. Psalms 42:5 says, "Why are you in despair, O my soul? And why have you become disturbed within me? Hope in God, for I shall again praise Him for the help of His presence." Always remember to be open, aware, and to cooperate with God as you walk toward healing day by day and moment by moment. To journey in this way allows you to experience the Presence of God and the wonder of life. Every step and breath will allow for your hope toward the future to unfold.

Let's begin your final day by taking time to align yourself spiritually with your affirmations, your God prayer, and your visualization/meditation. Be sure you are prepared to begin your writing for today with a pen and paper or a notebook/journal. Also, find a place that is comfortable and relaxing. Try to create a writing space that offers you serenity and peace by removing clutter and adjusting the temperature and lighting in the room to your preferences. Consider lighting a scented candle to enhance your creativity. Consider Orange, which can help to reduce anxiety. Cedar and Lavender scents are known to reduce tension, and Vanilla and Cinnamon-Vanilla scents are best known for calm and creativity.

This day will be different than previous days, because you will be expressing yourself through creativity and discovering another kind of writing activity. Today, you will write a poem. You are not expected to become a poet; so no worries here. This is just another way to express yourself. You will choose to write a poem on one of the following topics: death, your loved one, your emotions, from the heart of another person to their loved one, to Self, or to God. Carefully consider which topic you would like to express a message or poem for today. Your choice may be an indication of where most of your healing is needed and you can consider focusing your energy in this direction as you move forward each day.

Your poem doesn't have to rhyme, but if you notice your words are forming a rhyming pattern, allow the flow to move you through the process. The rhyming pattern may be a way for your spirit to remind you to find your rhythm in life once again. The source or creator of all that exists knows the most beneficial way to bring harmony to your life and spirit. All the words that flow through you as you write are your messengers of hope. This activity will allow you to balance the equilibrium that has shifted when you lost your loved one. It is in the quiet moments of writing each word that you will discover the harmony that is in your heart. This is the power of the unconscious mind being allowed to surface and create. Through openness and willingness, any form of creativity can serve as a way to heal and transform your life.

As you write your poem, start with a thought from your mind and write whatever your feeling in this place. Then, let your thoughts move to your heart, and listen for the words that your heart needs to express at this time. Your heart has a way of inputting signals from your brain and transmitting the lower thought patterns to higher thoughts of consciousness. It allows you to apply your divine vision toward your life circumstances. As Norman Vincent Peale said, "Change your thoughts and you change your world." When you change your thoughts your way of seeing the world changes—this is your divine vision.

In grief, it is vital to change the way you are thinking and seeing the world now that your loved one has passed, because your physical senses of connecting and exploring relationships has shifted and your inner sensibilities are now becoming active as you gain an awareness to the nature of spirit. With these new found senses your ability to create is more alive than ever before, so attempting to write creatively will allow you to purposely tune into your inner senses. If you would like guidance for this activity, you can reference the poems from the Heavenly Messages~ Forever In My Heart® collection for an example.

Let this be your time to be free and open to receive intuitive, creative guidance from within, and give your heart a voice with a message from spirit. Your poem will tell the story of moving through all your emotions, thoughts, and feelings of grief to a place of peace and inner knowing from divine presence. You can also choose to write how you feel about the last days you spent with your loved one, how you feel about having had been given the gift to share your life with them. This could be a message of gratitude, thanking your loved one for sharing their life with you. You will find that writing a thank you message to your loved one is a very healing and moving tribute to their life and all life. The message could be about your thoughts about not having them with you now, your feelings about the loss of a dream (this is a very real feeling when death occurs because the hopes and dreams we believed for the future have to now be transformed with a new way of hoping and dreaming), or any thought that is moving through you in regard to your loved one. This is your special time to create with your thoughts. So choose to write from a place that has the most emotional intensity.

You are taking your "self talk" of sorrow and diffusing it with your "spirit talk" of inspiration. The movement and flow of your writing today is very much the same as the previous days of writing, but now you are combining it all into one creative message. If you are gifted in music you can use these words as lyrics to a melody your heart has been waiting to create, or if you are a talented artist have these words inspire your hand to paint these emotional thoughts as on image onto the canvas. The poetry itself is an inspiring creation, but if your heart is leading you to create and use these feelings toward some other higher good through your gifts and talents, then please free yourself and allow the process of creativity to flow. Creativity is the greatest gift of healing. It allows you to actually see that something beautiful could be born from the sorrow and pain. There is great power in such a gift.

Through messaging and creative writing you are essentially evicting lower level thoughts from your being. The Messaging Process allows you to release yourself from the ownership of all your emotions, thoughts, and feelings of grief so that you can become free to dwell in the sacred dwelling of your soul as you heal. Each and every writing activity for the past fifteen days has been leading you to your ultimate reality and divinity so that you and God within can become the "soul proprietor" of your life.

Once you have finished your poem, consider offering a silent moment of prayer of gratitude for your divine message. Then, consider closing the process with your God Prayer. Take a few moments to breathe and sit quietly. Close your eyes and turn away from your outer world. You are relaxed and peaceful as you dwell within your inner presence of light. Allow the light to move through every part of your being. The light is healing, restoring, and maintaining your body, mind, and spirit. Through the light you can see yourself complete and whole. You envision yourself physically and emotionally healthy and peaceful doing all the things you love. You know that you carry eternal love and spirit within you every day. As you open your eyes your heart is full and your spirit renewed. You are ready to do this last activity to integrate your healing process.

Activity: The Messaging Process has allowed you to acknowledge your emotions and change your thoughts about them. Through grief you have seen dramatic changes in your life. These changes have propelled you toward transformation. Yet, it is the profound internal subtle shifts within your being that have required you to carve out a space for yourself so that you can be still to listen and be guided by your divine inner presence. With this process you have purified and detoxified your inner being with the truth and all that is whole, pure and good. You have cleansed your being through an emotional release process.

There are two activities to choose from today. Both offer closure and integrate healing of your experience for the fifteen days of messaging. For your first activity you will continue the purification process with an outdoor closing ceremony. For this activity you will need an outdoor open space that is safe, clear, and free from debris. You will also need wood for burning, buckets of water or a garden hose, and rocks to contain the fire. You are going to prepare a small outdoor fire or campfire. Please research the proper way to build a campfire so that you are well informed and prepared to do this activity without harm to yourself, others, or the environment. If you are under age, please ask an adult to facilitate and supervise your activity. There are many websites that offer information in regard to constructing a small campfire, so please do your homework.

Once your campfire is ready, you can begin the activity. You will be using the elements of fire and water as symbols of purity and spirit. With your messages in hand, you will sit quietly by the fire. Allow yourself to become centered and present with all the beauty of nature that is around you. Feel the warmth of the fire as it begins to offer you its fierce, purifying qualities. Quietly offer a prayer of gratitude and love to God for your healing.

You are now ready to begin. Please gather all your writings from the fifteen days of messaging and read them all to yourself. You will feel the intensity of your emotions as well as the power of spirit through each message. You will place your messages into the flaming light of the fire, and as you do, you will be symbolically purifying and unifying all your emotions. Consider saying the following affirmation as you place the papers into the glowing fire, "I release all negativity and trauma to the light, and I let all that is holy, good, and pure emanate to and through me, I let the embers glow in my heart eternally, I allow for this fire to purify my being and be a spark for my life. I am grateful for spirit, and I am one with God and all of eternity, and so it is." If there is another affirmation that resonates with you, feel free to say it at this time.

As the papers turn to ash and then to smoke you know that every thought, word, feeling, emotion is being sublimated to the light and to spirit. You are grounded, supported, renewed, and reborn through this purification process. Once the smoke has filled the air, and all the papers have been transmuted to spirit you will pour water over the campfire for safety but the element of water will symbolically awaken and cleanse your spirit with its pure and powerful nature. As the water distinguishes the fire, it is also cleansing and soothing your spirit.

Consider saying the following affirmation at this time: "I am whole and pure in spirit as this healing water washes away and distinguishes all negativity and trauma from my being, and so it is." Take a few deep breaths and remain quiet in your moment. You are calm, refreshed, and grateful for your experience. Close your ceremony with a silent prayer for you and your loved one.

If creating a campfire outdoors seems too difficult or there is inclement weather, consider the following activity. You will need scissors, a shoe box that you can decorate with beauty and creativity. Maybe paint some bright colors, add some ribbon, or write some healing words on the box, it is entirely your own personal expression for the way you would like to decorate the box. Next, gather all your messages and quietly read them to yourself to feel the emotional and spiritual intensity. Close your eyes, sit quietly and peacefully for a moment and go within the space of your heart for comfort and peace, offer a prayer of gratitude and love to God for your healing.

You are now ready to begin. Hold some of your messages in your hand and cut them into pieces with your scissors. Now do the same with the rest. You are symbolically cutting away all the junk that lived in side of you. Once you have all the paper cut into pieces, place them into your beautifully decorated box to symbolize the beauty of spirit that has been holding and carrying you through your grief experience. Seal the box with ribbon.

Consider saying the following affirmation: "I am whole and one with spirit and all that is eternal. I remove all negativity and trauma from within. It is the God of my being that holds, carries, and guides me throughout my life. I am safe, secure, and connected to the treasures within my heart, the eternal home of love. And so it is."

As you hold the box in your hands, close your eyes and offer a silent prayer for the person you were, the person you are now, and the person you are discovering through your healing journey. You feel strong, confident, renewed, and connected. Finally, you can consider taking the box outside and placing it into the ground. If you do this, make it a peaceful and spiritual experience as you symbolically return pieces of yourself to earth and spirit. Allow yourself to feel grounded and aligned with all that is spirit. Consider planting a beautiful, colorful plant to symbolize the resurrecting and birth of your new being. Close with a silent prayer for you and your loved one.

In closing our time together, I offer you my prayers, peace, and love.

It is important for you to know that now that you have completed your fifteen-day spiritual path toward healing from grief that your journey has only just begun. Since healing from grief is an everyday effort, I would strongly recommend doing the Messaging Process again for another fifteen days as you continue to heal. As mentioned earlier in this book, recent research suggests that a healthy pattern for thirty to forty days can provide a healing change in behavior that could benefit your life. You would be surprised to learn how many emotions and feelings are still present even when you think you have consciously worked through them all. Your willingness to reflect and journey through these unknown and known places of grief will serve as your guide as you shake off the debris of your past and step into the present moment.

Your healing journey requires that you travel lightly. Through the broken pieces of the heart there is an open path leading you to the unending flow of God's grace. There is no need to carry a heavy load of emotional baggage as you move on in your life. This will keep you stuck in negative, unhealthy thought patterns. Your focus is to remain on the open path and let the pieces fall into the hands of God. The inner dwelling of the divine constant will impart awareness to your emotions and circumstances as to provide you with the ability to walk uprightly and diligently in the days ahead. Remember that you are one with spirit and all you will ever need to carry are your loved ones and God in your heart every day. You are brave and you have strength to loosen the gripping hands of grief off your life and heart. Know and trust that each moment your grief is being released to a Higher Wisdom as you move toward healing.

The death experience teaches a very valuable lesson, to honor and respect life. As you travel on your journey, let your love and passion for life touch everyone you meet. Remember to cherish each person in your life and to live every moment with them as if it were your last, because you never know if you will be given the gift to hear their voice or see their face tomorrow. Whatever the circumstances, whether perceived as good or bad, embrace them all with grace and love knowing that "we shall never pass this way again." Let this be your legacy and make your life worth the trip.

My heart is with you as you make your way. Thank you for allowing me to share these moments with you.

All my love and blessings to you always.—Love, Debra Ann

Chapter 5

Heavenly Messages~ Forever In My Heart ® poems.

Messages to Heaven—poetic and inspirational
messages to your loved ones in heaven
A collection of a unique brand spiritual messages

Why love if losing hurts so much?
We love to know we are not alone.
—C.S. Lewis

Heavenly Messages for Children

A child's spirit is like a child. You can never catch it by running after it. You must stand still, and for love, it will soon itself come back.

—Arthur Miller

An Angel's Garden

There is a special place
That only God knows
A place inside a mother
Where a baby nourishes and grows
They begin life as a seed
Planted within their mother's womb
Carefully placed with God's gentle care
They miraculously bloom
But sometimes this perfect gift of life
Does not become a flower
Yet God gives His precious creation
A very spiritual power
He sends His loving arms
To gently carry away
A little angel up to heaven
To sing with praise all day
Although we're left never knowing
What this child may have been
God knew each had a purpose
So He called them home to Him
And as all the angels join together
To sing a heavenly tune
A angel's garden flourishes and grows
Eternally in bloom
Cultivated by all the little angels
Who now resound
In God's garden room
For as the garden grows
Each precious angel will adorn the choir
To triumphantly sing their part
While a flower blooms perpetually

In an angel's garden
And within our heart

My Child, My Precious Angel

For some, God gives a special gift
To bring to earth a child
And when this angel is created
Angels are entrusted to us for a while
The day you were born
We felt so very blessed to see your eyes and face
We counted all your fingers and toes
God had put all in its place
A perfect child to love each day
We felt tremendous joy
And on your very first day of lifeDaddy bought you your first toy
We watched you grow day by day
So excited to hear the first word you would say
And every day you would play and play
Your laughter was our song
But we never imagined that your music
Wouldn't last for much too long
The tears we cry, the pain we feel
Our hearts are forever broken
And though we try to get by
Few words are ever spoken
But then, one day, we held hands
And we heard your spirit say
Daddy and Mommy please don't cry
It was meant to be this way
So now, we're thankful for our angel that God gave
If only for a while
To know, to love, to watch grow
To see that precious smile
And every night we ask and pray
For God to hold you in His loving arms

To take care of you each day
And when He calls us home
To the heavens up above
We will stay together forever
In His eternal light and love
For now, through God's grace, there is a place
Where our love can never part
My precious angel, you will always be
Forever in my heart

My Child, My Heaven

My child, my heart is filled with pain to grieve
Since it does not seem natural for a child first to leave
If I could give my life to get you back today
I would surrender in a moment
To bring you back to stay
Your time here was not long enough
There was so much more to be
A future filled with hopes and dreams
All dashed by destiny
Yet, I know there are so many reasons to remember
The joy of having you
Your music, books, and the hobbies you loved
All the friends that you knew
Although my heart is broken
I still feel so very blessed
To have had a child who lived their life
With love and tenderness
And with all these feeling I hold deep inside
With so many loving thoughts of you
I have to pray for the faith to carry on
For the strength to press through
So every night I will ask and pray
For God to send His loving light my child's way
And hold you in His arms so strong
For it is in His tender care that you now belong
And I am thankful for the time we shared, if only for awhile
To know you, to love you, to watch you grow
You touched my life with your smile
For I know that God sent a piece of heaven down
When He gave your life to me
And it is to heaven that you have now returned

And I hope, with you, to one day be
But, for the moment, God keeps a place within
Where our love can never part
My beautiful child, you will always be
Forever in my heart

My Child, You Will Always Be

My child
My heart is filled with pain to grieve
Since it does not seem natural for our children first to leave
Especially when a child leaves so much of life behind
Your family, your friends and all of your work
The answers are hard to find
If I could only have you here
I would give most anything
To see your smile, or hear your voice
The joy that you would bring
When I see your family and friends without you
It makes my heart ache so
There was so much more to do together
To learn, to love, to grow
For now, I will hold on to the memories
Of my precious child
And the hope to one day be with you
Eases the sorrow for awhile
Now as I pray for strength and grace
To press through this way
I will thank God for the miracle
That touched my life each day
For I will always remember
How proud you made me
More than words could ever say
And as God holds you close
In His loving arms so dear
I will ask for His eternal light and peace
To keep you in His perfect care
But for the moment, God keeps a place within
Where our love can never part

My beautiful child, you will always be
Forever in my heart

To My Son, Shine

For every word we can no longer share
A tear is shed for you
For every moment no longer here
A tear is shed for you
For your smile that once turned
My dark sky blue
A tear is shed for you
For your life that was taken much too soon
A tear is shed for you
For all these tears that I shed
Only one prayer still remains
Please God, take hold of the tears I've cried
And wash away my pain
I no longer want to flood my eyes
With so much hurt and sorrow
I surrender my tears now to you
To shed light on my tomorrow
And if, My Beautiful Son
My tears have weighed you down
And your light through the darkness
I could not find
My eyes are now wiped clear to see
So let your spirit
Shine

To My Daughter, Shine

For every word we can no longer share
A tear is shed for you
For every moment no longer here
A tear is shed for you
For your smile that once turned
My dark sky blue
A tear is shed for you
For your life that was taken much too soon
A tear is shed for you
For all these tears that I shed
Only one prayer still remains
Please God, take hold of the tears I've cried
And wash away my pain
I no longer want to flood my eyes
With so much hurt and sorrow
I surrender my tears now to you
To shed light on my tomorrow
And if, My Beautiful Daughter
My tears have weighed you down
And your light through the darkness
I could not find
My eyes are now wiped clear to see
So let your spirit
Shine

The Angel of My Heart

God had given me a special gift
On that miraculous day you were born
He had manifested an angel
Here on earth in human form
And your little hand was created
To fit perfectly into mine
And your tender smile
Brought such love and joy
Only heaven could define
For God had given me precious gift
On that miraculous day you were born
But the beautiful angel He created
Has now returned to heavenly form
Yet, there is a place where my angel abides
For divine love can never part
My beautiful child
You will always be
The angel of my heart

My Child, One of God's Special Children

For some, we receive a blessing
A child intended from above
A special child from heaven
Filled with God's pure and humble love
When you were born
They said you were different
To some not quite the same
To us you were so very perfect
Because we knew from where you came
The lessons that you taught us
God's secrets to reveal
Through your gentle kindness and your love
You taught us how to feel
Yet, God set you apart
From your kind and all the rest
But this difference was the gift He gave
To His children He loved best
The special child who can touch your life
And teach you how to be
Not by words or the knowledge of this world
But by the way we feel and see
With a simple smile or a sweet embrace
With the love you had to give
His heavenly nature He had placed in you
God's own image through you lived
And although we are broken hearted
We still feel so very blessed
To had been given a child
Whose heart was made
With God's loving grace and goodness
So now we are thankful for our special child

God's own blessing in our hand
An angel so true on this earth
With divine love to understand
For God has called our angel home
To be in His eternal love and care
And one day we will be together
With eternity to share
But for now, God keeps a place within
Where our love will never part
My beautiful child
You are my soul
You're forever in my heart

Our Perfect Child

In every life God has a plan
From the moment we are conceived
As my child
God gave your life through me
A path was paved
His plan achieved
We never imagined your life to be different
You were a perfect child in every way
Then there seemed to be a sudden change of fate
On one very destined day
They said your challenge would be difficult
To some, no longer the same
To us, you were still that perfect child
Only more precious
Through your struggle and pain
The lessons that you taught us
God's secrets to reveal
Through your gentle kindness and your love
You taught us how to feel
With your challenge you touched our life
And taught us how to be
Not by words or the knowledge of this world
But by the way we feel and see
With a simple smile or a sweet embrace
With the love you had to give
His heavenly nature He had placed in you
God's own image through you lived
And although we are broken hearted
We still feel so very blessed
To had been given a child
Whose heart was created

With God's loving grace and goodness
And now we are thankful for our perfect child
God's own blessing in our hand
An angel so true on this earth
With divine love to understand
For God has called our angel home
To be in His eternal love and care
And one day we will be together
With eternity to share
But for now, God keeps a place within
Where our love will never part
My beautiful child, you are my soul
You're forever in my heart

Daughter-in-Law, You Will Always Be Our Family

You are a very special person
Because our son chose you to be
His partner for a lifetime
His true one and only
And when he made that choice
We knew you had become
A part of our family
Our hearts you had won
The time we shared together
We will not erase
Because within our family
You filled a special place
To us you will always be
Like a child of our own
And we feel so very blessed
And so privileged to have known
A person who was so loving, kind, and good
You were always willing to share our ways
You always understood
And so we know that God had given us
A special kind of child
A daughter, through marriage
God had loaned us
If only for awhile
And we are thankful to have had you in our lives
And please know we will never part
You will always be our family
You're forever in our heart

Son-in- Law, You Will Always Be Our Family

You are a very special person
Because our daughter chose you to be
Her partner for a lifetime
Her true one and only
And when she made that choice
We knew you had become
A part of our family
Our hearts you had won
The time we shared together
We will not erase
Because within our family
You filled a special place
To us you will always be
Like a child of our own
And we feel so very blessed
And so privileged to have known
A person who was so loving, kind, and good
You were always willing to share our ways
You always understood
And so we know that God had given us
A special kind of child
A son, through marriage
God had loaned us
If only for awhile
And we are thankful to have had you in our lives
And please know we will never part
You will always be our family
You're forever in our heart

Heavenly Messages for Parents

All that I am or hope to be I owe to my angel Mother —Abraham Lincoln

My father didn't tell me how to live; he lived and let me watch him do it. —Clarence Budington Kelland

To My Parents, with Gratitude and Love

My heart is filled with love and gratitude
For my Mom and Dad
God had given me two special people
The best parents a child could have
They taught me how to walk and talk
To blow a kiss and wave good bye
They always knew how to make me laugh
Whenever I would cry
And as I grew up they set an example
Of the kind of life I were to live
Not only by their actions
And words so wise
But through all the love they had to give
And although they believe they wanted a child
To love and watch grow
It was God who chose them to teach me
All the things in life I needed to know
So everything I am today
Or I hope to one day be
I owe with gratitude to my mother and father
Who gave more than life to me
They taught me to bring joy to sorrow
To keep my head held high
To always hope for a bright tomorrow
To embrace each moment that passes by
And I am thankful for these lessons
They are what I hold so dear
Mom and Dad, I need to apply them now
To my life without you here
That is why my heart is filled
With sincere thanks and love

An expression intended for my beautiful parents
Who now listen from above
So I thank you both for your strength and love
You taught me to endure
All these words are inscribed upon my heart
I will love you forevermore

My Mother, the Hands of Time

When I was young, you would hold my hand
And gently lead the way
Within your grip I knew
Your love was here to stay
You gave your love unselfishly
With a heart so true
Whenever I needed a safe place to fall
I could always turn to you
The years had passed
Time had reversed
Your hand now held in mine
I hope that I gave you love
The same unselfish kind
I prayed for God to keep you here
Forever and a day
Yet, I have to trust His infinite plan
The time to go or stay
For the Lord has called you home
To relieve you from your fight
He has reached out His gentle hands to lead you
Into His eternal love and light
And He has carried you to a better place
Where all the angels hold your hand
And I hope that there you will rest in peace
Until we meet again
For now, God provides a place within
Where our love will never part
He has eternally joined my hand with yours
Forever in my heart

My Mother, My Treasured Memory

When I was a child
There was a song
My mother sang, especially for me
She would take my hands
And hold me tight
Within her melody
Held in her arms
I was lifted up
Her song became a dance
Spinning around
We laughed with joy
This moment not by chance
For I remember her special song
The tune and words
Still play
Her melody sings within my heart
To never fade away
And that moment still lifts me up
Her dance and song
God's gift to me
The eternal music of my heart
My treasured memory
For I will always hold close to her in spirit
And never will we part
My beautiful mother
You will always be
Forever in my heart

My Mother—The Heart of an Angel

A mother's heart is a perfect gift of love
An angel's touch sent to us from the heavens above
Within her heart you can believe
That God had taken special care
To create for every person
An angel that is so very dear
To love, guide, and protect us
And devote all of her time
He gave her a special grace
A privilege so divine
The ability to love us
With the heart of no other
He sent this angel down to earth
Where she became a mother
Then, when God calls a mother's heart
To return to her angelic place
He creates a bond between mother and child
That time cannot erase
For there is a place between heaven and earth
Where each of their love still clings
And it is found within the loving heart of a mother
Beneath her gentle sheltered wings
So, I thank you Mom for all your love, and please know
Our love will never part
As my mother, you are God's special angel
You're forever in my heart

To My Mom, With a Heart of Gratitude and Love

How many times should a child say
Thank you
To their mother for all her love
For the gift of life she gave to you
How she gently held your hand
For the words she wisely shared with you
Knowing alone you did not stand
For the strength she kindly demonstrated
As a mother and a friend
How she knew your joys and sorrows
Knowing on her you could depend
How many times should a child say
Thank you
To their mother for all her love
Especially when it is intended for her
In the heavens up above
Thank you is not a sentiment that can be measured
By counting the words that are spoken
But more possibly by the measure
That lies within the heart
In the bits and pieces of the broken
For it is in the heart that one can find
Eternal gratitude and love
Since it speaks directly to a divine place
My mother
Now at peace in the heavens above
So I thank you Mom, for all your love
Which words alone cannot impart
For my gratitude and love are always
Forever in my heart

To My Mother, My Precious Moments

The moments I have of you
I will cherish everyday
And I will always hold them in a place
Where time won't let them fade away
For there were times when all I needed
Was your hand to shelter mine
There were times when I looked up at you
To search for the pride I couldn't find
There were times when your smile told me
That everything would be all right
Because I knew in your eyes
I was perfect in your sight
Now all these memories hold a sacred place
Between heaven and my soul
Now these moments in time
Complete and make me whole
And every time I think of you
Your light radiates my heart
And I am shining in your presence
Within this moment we are not apart
And as I carry each precious moment
Throughout my life I'll see
The tender gift God gave
Through a loving memory

A Mother's Love

A mother's love is like a river
That runs so strong and deep
It's the kind of love so precious
Your soul needs it to keep

But when it is gone from our embrace
Sometimes life is hard to handle
And it seems that her love has been blown away
Like a kiss from the wind on a candle

And within the swirling cloud of smoke
In the dark air now left behind
Seems to dwell only our melting tears
When it seems her love is hard to find
Yet a waterfall of tears
Can never replace the steady flow
Of a mother's river of love
That eternally lights
A candle's glow

My Father, My Strength

When I was young we would go for walks
And you would take me to the park
In my room, when I was afraid
You were my light throughout the dark
You gave your love with strength and grace
Always knowing which was best
You taught me to respect myself
To be different from the rest
Your courage and support gave hope to us
Through difficult times and good
Always with a sense of pride
With dignity you stood
You kept everything inside yourself
Securely locked away
With a smile and your loving words
You knew just what to say
Now the years have passed
And time will not erase
The tower of strength you will always be
But now, I ask if for awhile
You pass that strength to me
For the Lord has called you home
To relieve you from your fight
It is time for you now to rest
In His eternal peace and light
And please know, for now, God keeps a place within
Where our love will never part
Thank you Dad, for your love and strength
You're forever in my heart

For My Dad, My Secret Wish

When I was a child
My father would carry me
High on top of his shoulders
Often at times when we would both play
I was his pal
I would always say
And I remember I made a secret wish
That it will always be this way
But then, one day, my world stood still
And I realized my wish
God could not fill
And the shoulders that once carried me
Are now a treasured memory
A single moment
Stuck in time
A stolen glance
Into my heart and mind
Yet in this place I am so aware
That God had granted my wish
That was so dear
To remember you, Dad
Your smile and face
Your laughter and words
Your warm embrace
And with each thought
I can feel you near
So when I pray
These words you can hear
That now, God carry you on His shoulders
And lift you way on high
And raise you up into the heavens

Where all the angels fly
And please know although we are not together
Our love can never part
My loving Dad, till we meet again
You're forever in my heart

To My Father, My Precious Moments

The moments I have of you
I will cherish everyday
And I will always hold them in a place
Where time won't let them fade away
For there were times when all I needed
Was your hand to shelter mine
There were times when I looked up at you
To search for the pride I needed to find
There were times when your smile told me
That everything would be all right
Because I knew in your eyes
You held my reflection
And I was perfect in you sight
Now without you here I realize
God had given me a gift of love
He sent His goodness through my father
With precious memories
From above

To My Dad, With a Heart of Gratitude and Love

How many times should a child say
Thank you
To their father for all his love
For the gift of life he gave to you
How he carried you so strong
For the sacrifices made for you
So that nothing would go wrong
How he guided you with a gentle hand
And shared all his thoughts so wise
How you always felt loved and protected
When you looked into his eyes
How many times should a child say
Thank you
To their father for all his love
Especially when it is intended for him
In the heavens up above
Thank you is not a sentiment that can be measured
By counting the words that are spoken
But more possibly by the measure
That lies within the heart
In the bits and pieces of the broken
For it is in the heart that one can find
Eternal gratitude and love
Since it speaks directly to a divine place
My father
Now at peace in the heavens above
So I thank you Dad, for all your love
Which words alone cannot impart
For my gratitude and love are always
Forever in my heart

The Love of a Father

The love of a father is strong and proud
Yet gentle enough to confide
The love of a father protects and shelters
When standing by your side
The love of a father encourages and guides
But never controls your way
The love of a father forms a child
To become what they are today
All the love you gave you to me
Lives strong within my mind
And when I'm lost
I only need to search my heart
It is there your love I'll find
And in this place
Your love remains
With every moment that we shared
And it covers me and comforts me
With all your tender loving care
And I am guided by your light
As if you were holding my hand
An eternal touch sent from heaven
Because God knows
Only a father can understand
And here I know the truth
We can never be apart
The love of a father is overflowing
Forever in my heart

To My Mother-in-Law, Thank You for Your Love

There is a special woman
Sometimes life gives us the privilege to know
She is a kind and loving person
Who held your spouse's hand
And gave them love to grow
At first she was the only one
The center of her children's life
Until her little boy became a husband
Or her little girl became a wife
As her children reached a mature age
Her heart she had to hide
For the love of her babies
She always kept, locked away inside
Then, through a special bond of marriage
The name mother began to mean so much more
So she learned to expand her love and give herself
To become a mother-in law
And with the same love
She gave to her own
So tender and so true
She freely gave to another's child
And made them her family too
So through marriage
God had given me
Someone else's mother to adore
A special woman in her own child's life
Who became my mother-in-law
So I thank you for your child
Who you and I both love
And I know you're watching over us
From the heavens up above

And though right now we are not together
We will never be apart
Thank you for all your love
You're forever in my heart

To My Father-in-Law, With Gratitude

There is a special man
Sometimes life gives us the privilege to know
He is a strong and caring person
Who guided your spouse
And gave them love to grow
At first he was the only one
The center of his children's life
Until his baby boy became a husband
Or his little girl became a wife
Then, through a special bond of marriage
The name father began to mean so much more
So he opened his arms and heart
To become a father-in law
And with the same love
He gave to his own
So true and so strong
He freely gave to another's child
For in his family, they too belonged
So through marriage
God had given me
Someone else's father to adore
A special man in his own child's life
Who became my father-in-law
So I thank you for your strength and caring
That you gave with respect and love
And I know you're watching over us
From the heavens up above
And though right now we are not together
We will never be apart
To my father-in-law, with sincere gratitude
You're forever in my heart

Heavenly Messages for Husband and Wife

I love thee, I love but thee. With love that shall not die. Till the sun grows cold, and the stars grow old. —Baynard Taylor

To My Husband

I wish I could tell you one more time
How wonderful you made my life

I wish I could tell you one more time
I was so proud to be your wife

I wish I could tell you one more time
I cherished every moment we shared

I wish I could tell you one more time
How much for you I cared

For all these words
I am wishing to say
I know you still can hear
For they are whispered
Through the loving gift of our family
Everyday
To you, my Dear

My Husband, My One True Love

As we sailed together
Through this journey we call life
I was so very blessed to be
Your best friend and your wife
You were the one person who knew and shared
All my thoughts and dreams
Through your words, a glance, your gentle touch
I had it all it seemed
It is so hard to get along
Without you here with me
There was so much more we had to do
So much we planned to see
Growing old together
To enjoy our family
But sometimes our plans don't always follow through
So I'll try my best to give my all
On what we planned to do
With God's love, strength, and providence
I hope I'll find my place
But, right now, my most tender prayer
Is for you dear
To rest within His loving grace
And because He gave us the gift
Of our love
I know that I can reach
To the heavens up above
And there I will be able to find
The faith that I can depend
So I can pray for your soul to rest
And for my heart to mend

For I know that you are with the Lord
In His presence so divine
And once again, we will be together
And there will be no measure of time
But, if for the moment, we both must be apart
You will always be my one true love
You're forever in my heart

My Husband, My Dream Come True

So often year after year
I find myself wishing
More and more that you were here
For when I see the beauty
We both created in this life
I see a reflection of the love we shared
As a husband and a wife
I am tenderly reminded
Of all the dreams we saw come true
And I am inspired that your love
Still gives me the strength to awaken
All the dreams within I never knew
For your love is still here with me
It no longer seem so far away
And my wish for you to be with me still
Has come true with the rise of each new day
For I will always hold a dream within my heart
That belongs to just us two
To be together forever
A loving wish, my dream come true

The Gift of Love

There is a special man
Who God sent to me with love
A man who became my husband
A gift from up above
More than just a man
My closest friend, my soul
My inspiration, my every thought
With him my life was whole
Together we planned a future
Our hopes and dreams to come
Now I am facing our plans alone
Yet with his spirit, I am more than one
For I know that this special man
That God sent as my other half
Taught me the importance of life
To live, to love, to laugh
And the gift that I was given
My husband, my best friend
Is my eternal hope and treasure
That our love will have no end
For only the gift of love
Can transcend the boundaries
That keeps heaven and earth apart
My dearest love, till we meet again
You're forever in my heart

The One I Love, My Destiny

When we first met I knew
You were the one for me
I looked into your eyes
And I found my destiny
Together we shared all our hopes
Our dreams and plans
But now it seems like all our thoughts
Were written in the sands
And everything just slipped away
And passed right through my hands
That is how I feel right now
Without you here with me
Without your strength and love
I don't know how to be
At times like this I wish
That I could hold your hand
Or talk with you
And search your eyes
To help me understand
I feel as though I can hear your voice
Telling me to be strong
And although you can't be with me
That it is here that I belong
So for now, I will pray to seek an inner place
Where our loving God can carry me
And send His peace and grace
Because when we grieve the loss
Of those we love so dear
That is the time we know
Our Lord is always near
For when He calls me home

On that final day
I know that you will be waiting
And together we will stay
But for now, God provides a place within
Where we can never part
I will love you for eternity
You're forever in my heart

To My Wife

I wish I could tell you one more time
How wonderful you made my life

I wish I could tell you one more time
I was so proud you were my wife

I wish I could tell you one more time
I cherished every moment we shared

I wish I could tell you one more time
How much for you I cared

For all these words
I am wishing to say
I know you still can hear
For they are whispered
Through the loving gift of our family
Everyday
To you, my Dear

My Wife, My One True Love

As we sailed together
Through this journey we call life
I was so very blessed to have you
For my best friend and my wife
The one person who knew and shared
All my thoughts and dreams
Through your words, a glance, your gentle touch
I had it all it seemed
It is so hard to get along
Without you here with me
There was so much more we had to do
So much we planned to see
Growing old together
To enjoy our family
But sometimes our plans don't always follow through
So I'll try my best to give my all
On what we planned to do
With God's love, strength, and providence
I hope I'll find my place
But, right now, my most tender prayer
Is for you dear
To rest within His loving grace
And because He gave us the gift
Of our love
I know that I can reach
To the heavens up above
And there I will be able to find
The faith that I can depend
So I can pray for your soul to rest
And for my heart to mend

For I know that you are with the Lord
In His presence so divine
And once again, we will be together
And there will be no measure of time
But, if for the moment, we both must be apart
You will always be my one true love
You're forever in my heart

My Wife, My Dream Come True

So often year after year
I find myself wishing
More and more that you were here
For when I see the beauty
We both created in this life
I see a reflection of the love we shared
As a husband and a wife
I am tenderly reminded
Of all the dreams we saw come true
And I am inspired that your love
Still gives me the strength to awaken
The dreams within I never knew
Now every wish for you
No longer seems so distant
And my love for you still forever strong
For I will always keep
A dream within my heart
Where only you belong

The Gift of Love

There is a special woman
Who God brought to me with love
A woman who became my wife
A gift from up above
More than just a woman
My closest friend, my soul
My inspiration, my every thought
With her my life was whole
Together we planned a future
Our hopes and dreams to come
Now I am facing our plans alone
Yet with her spirit, I am more than one
For I know that this special woman
That God sent as my other half
Taught me the importance of life
To live, to love, to laugh
And the gift that I was given
My wife, my best friend
Is my eternal hope and treasure
That our love will have no end
For only the gift of love
Can transcend the boundaries
That keeps heaven and earth apart
My dearest love, till we meet again
You're forever in my heart

The One I Love, My Destiny

When we first met I knew
You were the one for me
I looked into your eyes
And I found my destiny
Together we shared all our hopes
Our dreams and plans
But now it seems like all our thoughts
Were written in the sands
And everything just slipped away
And passed right through my hands
That is how I feel right now
Without you here with me
Without your strength and love
I don't know how to be
At times like this I wish
That I could hold your hand
Or talk with you
And search your eyes
To help me understand
I feel as though I can hear your voice
Telling me to be strong
And although you can't be with me
That it is here that I belong
So for now, I will pray to seek an inner place
Where our loving God can carry me
And send His peace and grace
Because when we grieve the loss
Of those we love so dear
That is the time we know
Our Lord is always near
For when He calls me home

On that final day
I know that you will be waiting
And together we will stay
But for now, God provides a place within
Where we can never part
I will love you for eternity
You're forever in my heart

Heavenly Messages for Sister and Brother

To the outside world we grow old. But not to brothers and sisters. We know each other as we always were. We know each other's hearts. We share private family jokes. We remember family feuds and secrets, family griefs and joys. We live outside the touch of time. —Clara Ortega

A sibling may be the keeper of one's identity, the only person with the keys to one's unfettered, more fundamental self. —Marian Sandmaier

My Sister, My Best Friend

When we were little
The two of us would laugh and play all day
And I thought it was so wonderful
To have my best friend here to stay
As we grew older
The years went by
It was on each other we would rely
For a sister holds a special friendship
A place where you can go
Where you're not afraid to be yourself
To let your feelings show
With a happy laugh
And a generous smile, there were times of joy to share
Or a heartfelt cry
With tears to dry and long talks to show we care
But then, there came a time
For God to call you home
And now there is emptiness
I feel so all alone
So as I walk without you
I'll take life day by day
And when I think about you
It is this prayer that I will say
That God keep you in His special place
Where all the angels rest
I am thankful for my sister
My one true friend, my best
For now, God keeps a place within
Where our love will never part
My sister, my friend
Till we meet again
You're forever in my heart

My Brother, My One True Friend

When we were younger
We had each other
To keep us safe and sound
In my heart
I could always count on you
You would never let me down
We shared our laughter together with good times
When times were hard we held strong
I never doubted you were a true friend
You taught me to belong
And that special bond between us
Through all the years held true
But shared moments
Become precious memories
A time to treasure
Between me and you
Now as I walk without you
I'll take life day by day
And when I think about you
It is this prayer that I will say
That God keep you in his loving arms
And hold you like no other
You were the person that I could always depend
My one true friend, my brother
And please know that God keeps a place within
Where we both can never part
I love you, till we meet again
You're forever in my heart

More Than a Sister-in-Law

When marriage made us family
I knew that you would be
More than a sister-in-law
You were a friend to me
A genuine smile always graced your face
With you there was no pretend
And when I needed a helping hand
You were always there to lend
And through marriage, you became a sister
Someone I could always depend
It was fate that brought us closer
From sister-in-laws to friends
So, I know that I will miss you
And while I'm here I'll pray
To ask God, now, to lend his hand
For it is in His eternal care you will stay
And I am thankful to have you in my family
To fill a special part
As my "sister" and always my friend
You're forever in my heart

More Than a Brother-in-Law

When marriage made us family
I knew that you would be
More than a brother-in-law
You were a friend to me
A tender heart you gave to all
With you there was no pretend
And when I needed a helping hand
You were always there to lend
And through marriage, you became a brother
Someone I could always depend
It was fate that brought us closer
From brother-in-laws to friends
So, I know that I will miss you
And while I'm here I'll pray
To ask God, now, to lend his hand
For it is in His eternal care you will stay
And I am thankful to have you in my family
To fill a special part
As my "brother" and always my friend
You're forever in my heart

Heavenly Messages for Grandchild

If I know what love is, it is because of you." —Hermann Hesse

My Granddaughter, A Perfect Gift of Love

There is a special child
Whom I prayed to know one day
A child that I could hold and love
And pass the time with play
This child is my granddaughter
A true blessing from above
God's creation manifested through our own child
A perfect gift of love
And our granddaughter that God gave us
Filled us with overwhelming joy and pride
But now without your tender smile
There is only sadness deep inside
And since I prayed to have you here
To love and watch you grow
I am so thankful for the time we shared
For the granddaughter I loved so
And I know the Lord had blessed us
To show His love in such a way
For with the same love
His eternal light will shine
To guide you home to stay
But for now, God keeps a place within
Where our love will never part
My precious granddaughter, you will always be
Forever in my heart

My Granddaughter, My Joy

There is a special child
Whom I prayed to know one day
A child who brought so much joy
More than words could ever say
This child is my granddaughter
A true blessing from above
God's creation manifested through our own child
A perfect gift of love
And our granddaughter that God gave us
Filled us with overwhelming love and pride
But now without your tender smile
There is only sadness deep inside
And since I prayed to have you here
To know and watch you grow
I am so thankful for the time we shared
For the granddaughter I loved so
And I know the Lord had blessed us
To show His love in such a way
For with the same love
His eternal light will shine
To guide you home to stay
But for now, God keeps a place within
Where our love will never part
My precious granddaughter, you will always be
Forever in my heart

My Grandson, A Perfect Gift of Love

There is a special child
Whom I prayed to know one day
A child that I could hold and love
And pass the time with play
This child is my grandson
A true blessing from above
God's creation manifested through our own child
A perfect gift of love
And our grandson that God gave us
Filled us with overwhelming joy and pride
But now without your tender smile
There is only sadness deep inside
And since I prayed to have you here
To love and watch you grow
I am so thankful for the time we shared
For the grandson I loved so
And I know the Lord had blessed us
To show His love in such a way
For with the same love
His eternal light will shine
To guide you home to stay
But for now, God keeps a place within
Where our love will never part
My precious grandson, you will always be
Forever in my heart

My Grandson, My Joy

There is a special child
Whom I prayed to know one day
A child who brought so much joy
More than words could ever say
This child is my grandson
A true blessing from above
God's creation manifested through our own child
A perfect gift of love
And our grandson that God gave us
Filled us with overwhelming love and pride
But now without your tender smile
There is only sadness deep inside
And since I prayed to have you here
To know and watch you grow
I am so thankful for the time we shared
For the grandson I loved so
And I know the Lord had blessed us
To show His love in such a way
For with the same love
His eternal light will shine
To guide you home to stay
But for now, God keeps a place within
Where our love will never part
My precious grandson, you will always be
Forever in my heart

Heavenly Messages for Grandparents

We loved with a love that was more than love. —Edgar Allan Poe

My Grandmother, A Blessing in My Life

A grandmother is a special gift
Given to us from the heavens above
She is always there to give
Her complete and perfect love
She knows God has given her a blessing
So divine
To see her children's children grow
And share with them her time
For there were times when you would hold me close
And all my fears were chased away
There were times when I would run to you
And in your arms I hoped to stay
There were times when all I needed
Was your smile to make things right
For I knew that when you looked at me
I was perfect in your sight
Now without you here I realize
That God had blessed me more than you
He had given me His unconditional love
Through my grandmother
In her heart so true
So for now, there will always be a place within
Where our love will never part
I thank you Grandma, till we meet again
You're forever in my heart

To My Grandmother, My Precious Moments

The moments I have of you
I will cherish everyday
And I will always hold them in a place
Where time won't let them fade away
For there were times when all I needed
Was your hand to shelter mine
There were times when I looked up at you
To search for the pride I needed to find
There were times when your smile told me
That everything would be all right
Because I knew in your eyes
You held my reflection
And I was perfect in your sight
Now without you here I realize
God had given me a gift of love
He sent His goodness through my grandmother
With precious memories
From above

My Grandfather, A Blessing in my Life

A grandfather is a special person
Whose heart is so sincere
He is always willing to share his time
To laugh, to talk, to care
And when I was young
This wonderful man
Seemed so strong and tall
And his life within our family
Throughout the years
Gave love and wisdom to us all
Through actions and words
His character was revealed in many ways
And in every story he would tell
He always seemed so strong and brave
But underneath all his strength
There was a tender side
And he was always there to encourage
With a sense of love and pride
So now, I feel so very blessed
To have been given a grandfather like you
And I know you're watching over me
And everything I do
But for the moment, God provides a place within
Where our love will never part
Thank you for your goodness and strength
You're forever in my heart

To My Grandfather, My Precious Moments

The moments I have of you
I will cherish everyday
And I will always hold them in a place
Where time won't let them fade away
For there were times when all I needed
Was your hand to shelter mine
There were times when I looked up at you
To search for the pride I needed to find
There were times when your smile told me
That everything would be all right
Because I knew in your eyes
You held my reflection
And I was perfect in your sight
Now without you here I realize
God had given me a gift of love
He sent His goodness through my grandfather
With precious memories From above

Heavenly Messages for Niece, Nephew, and Cousin

The love we give away is the only love we keep.—Elbert Hubbard

My Precious Niece

There is a precious child
Who touched my life with love
A child who was like my own
A gift from up above

She filled my heart with laughter
There was so much joy within her smile
Though I believed
She was learning from me
She was teaching me
All the while

And the beauty that I learned to share
Were gifts of love, joy and peace
They had all been sent to me
Through a precious child
Who God created
To be my niece

For I will hold her close in spirit
To never be apart
My precious niece
You will always be
Forever in my heart

For My Nephew

There is a precious child
Who touched my life with love
A child who was like my own
A gift of life from up above

He filled my life with laughter
There was so much joy within his smile
Though I believed
He was learning from me
He was teaching me
All the while

And the gifts that I learned to share
To love with joy
To be always true
Had been sent to me
Through a precious child
Who God created
To be my nephew

For I will hold close to him in spirit
To never be apart
My precious nephew
You will always be
Forever in my heart

My Cousin, My Childhood Friend

I remember growing up together
Sharing memories and dreams
I remember private jokes and holidays
And all our childish schemes
I remember every time we shared
Our laughter and our tears
I remember the joy to have you with me
As we traveled through the years
And my Dear Cousin, I am grateful for those memories
And the beauty that they hold
Because every memory that visits me
Allows your spirit to unfold
And then I know you are with me
Sharing our love once again
I will always carry you in my heart
My Dear Cousin, My Childhood Friend

Heavenly Messages for Aunt and Uncle

Love must be as much a light as it is a flame.—Henry David Thoreau

To My Loving Aunt

You were always a special person
With whom I could share most anything
And I could always find a tender place
In our talks
Or just listening
There were times when I needed to know
Someone else was always there
And so you stood, my loving Aunt
With open arms to show you care
So I wish to truly thank you
For all your love that touched my life each day
And I know that you are still here with me
Our tender place won't fade away
For I will hold you close in spirit
To never be apart
My loving Aunt, you will always be
Forever in my heart

To My Loving Uncle

You were always a special person
With whom I could share most anything
And I could always find wisdom and strength
In our talks
Or just listening
There were times when I needed to know
Someone else was always there
And so you stood, my loving Uncle
With a strong shoulder to show you care
So I wish to truly thank you
For all your love that touched my life each day
And I know that you are still here with me
Your strength and words won't fade away
For I will hold you close in spirit
To never be apart
My loving Uncle, you will always be
Forever in my heart

Heavenly Messages for Friend, Someone Special, Hero, and Pet

"Love is, above all, the gift of oneself.—Jean Anouilh

My True Friend You Will Always Be

When we first met I knew
That I had found a friend in you
I knew you were a special person
So kind and always true
Through all the years we had together
We shared so many things
The joy, the talks, and the tears we cried
Who knew what life would bring
And though we took the bad times
Along with all the good
You were always standing by my side
Just like a good friend should
Now without you here with me
There is an empty space
But I know that you are in heaven
Because God has created a special place
For friends who are so true to us
He knows why they are here
To provide us with His divine love
That is why they are so dear
So, if for the moment, we both must be apart
My true friend you will always be
You're forever in my heart

To Someone Special

There are special people
That we meet only once in a lifetime
They have a gentle smile
And a generous heart
Their magic seems to shine
And when we are in their presence
We feel like we've been blessed
Because we are aware
We have encountered a spirit
That is different from the rest
For me you were that special person
Who touched my life in such a way
Your laughter and joy shined like the sun
To brighten every day
And because you were a star
That illuminated love
There will always be a warm embrace
A blanket from above
So I thank you for your joyful spirit
A soul so dignified
And I hope that when we meet again
You'll be my angel on the other side
But right now while I am here
I will miss your special spark
You have touched my life with your light
You're forever in my heart

To Our Heroes, We Are Forever Grateful

God created special people
Whose work is to save and give
They often risk their own lives
For many of us to live
When they chose their work
The Lord made it very clear
That on this path
He would bless them
With a loving heart to care
They wear a kind of uniform
Some say they look the same
But the Lord knows that they are different
And he calls each by their name
He also knows how well they serve
By the help that each one brings
So He equipped them divinely
And adorned each one with wings
And when these silent angels
With their lives do pay
They soar up to the heavens
To be heralded for their way
And we are aware that they are in a place
God carefully reserved
For all His special children
Those who so faithfully served
And as He lovingly holds them
For their eternal rest
We are forever grateful
Our heroes, we will not forget

My Pet, Tender Love

My family pet is a part of my family
In a very special way
Bringing joy into my heart
As I watch them run and play
Their love is unconditional
Some say they are man's best friend
Their eyes are so convincible
With all the love they send
And with the loyalty and trust
They always seem to give
I can only hope to share
In all the years they live
But when a family pet is called home
To a peaceful place above
I am forever grateful
To have received
All their tender love

Heavenly Messages for Every Heart

Love is a promise, love is a souvenir, once given never forgotten, never let it disappear —John Lennon

Do I Make You Proud?

So many words were left unsaid
Each held inside my heart and mind
Now the words are drenched with silent tears
Unanswered questions just rewind
Did you know how much I loved you
With every part of my soul
Can you see the emptiness inside my heart
From a place that once was whole
Are you looking down upon us
Through all the good and bad
Do you know when I am happy
Can you help me when I'm sad
Do you hear my silent wish
For just one more day with you
Do you know you're still a part
Of everything I say and do
So many unanswered questions
Yet somehow I still go on
I wonder what it is
That helps me stay so strong
Finally, I realize there is an answer
I feel you guiding me right now
And when I ask you everyday
Do I make you proud
I just look around and see
You're part of everything I am
And I no longer need to say another word
Or ask a question once again

The Knowing

Did you know that I was with you standing by your side?
Did you know that I was listening and wiped all the tears that you cried?
Did you know my arms were holding you every time you turned away?
Did you know my words were speaking with you pleading for you to stay?
Did you know that there was light shining through your darkest hour?
Did you know that within your heart you hold immeasurable strength and power?
The knowing is the gift that is given to anyone who seeks
No matter if you're standing strong or crumbled from defeat
But for those who thought that in their life they were fighting their battle all alone
God whispers, My child I am always here
And I will carry you safely home
Know that you were never lost
If only you had known

Dream Keeper

Each night before I fall asleep
I pray to have a dream to keep
Sometimes I see you in the distance
At an unfamiliar place
As I call out your name
My heart is quickly pounding
For the chance to see your face
Then I run to you
And reach out my hands
To pull you close to me
Only to pull away just little
To make sure it is you I see
As I hold your face in the palm of my hands
We both begin to smile
And we share a walk, a talk
And spend some time
So we can visit for a while
Then I awake from my dream
And I don't recall the details all too much
But I can remember your tender smile
Your beautiful eyes
And feeling your gentle touch
So tonight I'll say another prayer
To spend my night with you
And as I close my eyes to dream
You will be waiting for me too
And once again I hope to awake
With a special dream to keep
And look forward to the night
So I can see you when I sleep

Thinking of You

You came into my thoughts today
As you always do
And I can't help but to wonder
If where you are
Can you think about me too
You came into my thoughts today
And it seems like all has changed
At times against our will
My life and my world has rearranged
But in my mind
Time is standing still
You came into my thoughts today
And I wished I could hold you hand
Or see your smile or hear your voice
I am sure you would understand
You came into my thoughts today
And I began to cry
Because I miss you so much
And I want you here
So I wonder why
You came into my thoughts today
And I asked God to help me through
Suddenly I realized
There is really nothing I can do
All the tears I cry and the pain I feel
Will never bring you here
So I will remember that from now on
My thoughts of you
Will become my special prayer
You came into my thoughts today
And I began to smile

Because I know that when I think of you
We are together for a while
You came into my thoughts today
THANK YOU

Since You Left So Suddenly

How you left so suddenly
Without a reason why
We never even had the chance
To say our last good-bye
There wasn't time to hold your hand
Or to touch your sweet face
Nor a chance to say I love you
With a warm embrace
Now with these feelings
I find it hard to let go of you
Because when you passed so suddenly
A part of me left that day too
And though it seems like life
Seems so unfair and strange
I know it was your time
A moment in time that cannot be changed
Now all the heavenly angels
Wait for you
To return home through His door
For they know that though you were needed here
There you are needed more
Yet, I will never understand
Why life takes its turns and bends
But I know that when we meet in heaven
I'll be with you once again
For since you left so suddenly
With these words we will depart
Goodbye for now, I love you
You're forever in my heart

Till We Meet Again

A voice softly speaks inside of me
It fills my heart with tears
It whispers for me to say good-bye
To a life of times we've shared
This voice inside seems so quiet
Because the outside seems so loud
With all the people moving about their lives
Sounds of laughter from the crowd
And I feel like I am stuck in time
Between what once was and what is now
And my world has somehow silently stopped
Causing me to lowly bow
To all this pain and sorrow
I feel without you here
I know there will be tomorrow
Another day I hope to bear
But when the world outside is busy
And I am left standing still in place
God is waiting there to touch my heart
And fill my empty space
To lift me from the place I bowed
For He knows from where I fell
To encourage me and comfort me
With not another day to dwell
For good-bye is only a sentiment
The words my mind can hear
But the Lord consoles my heart
To mute the echo of farewell
Till we meet again, My Dear

A Time To Heal

As time goes on without you
The pain becomes so hard to bear
They say that wounds all heal in time
But I don't believe that is true
Because I can feel my wound bleeding
Each time I think of you
But now, I have had to learn
That it is not time
That heals the ache and grief
But how I use that time
To bring about relief
So all this pain and sadness
I feel from year to year
I will surrender to my Heavenly Father
To place his eternal care
And only then
Can I truly mend
The wound that cut so deep
So I can pray for your soul to rest
For it in God's loving arms you will sleep
And as time goes on without you here
I will gently make it through
Because is God is holding my hand
As he carries you

Heavenly Messages—Christian Messages

Love is a symbol of eternity. It wipes out all sense of time, destroying all memory of a beginning and all fear of an end. —Author Unknown

At The Cross

When I feel broken
And torn down from this loss
I kneel before Jesus
And I bow at the cross
When sorrow defeats me
With a powerful force
I kneel before Jesus
And I bow at the cross
At the cross there is compassion
For all of my pain
Through the suffering of Jesus
I break loose from this chain
He frees me from anger
From sadness and dread
By the wounds on His body
With the blood that He shed
For through His passionate death
Eternal life He had gave
To those who believe
For all to be saved
So as I kneel before Jesus
As I bow at the throne
I give praise to the Lord
For all those He's brought home
And I know you are with Him
In His glory you share
Now the cross that I carry
Seems lighter to bear
For again I will see you
With my creator, my source
And I will kneel before Jesus
I will bow at the cross

The Distance

There is a distance between us
That can only be measured by love
For one can never measure
The miles between earth
And the heavens above
But when the Lord stretched out his arms
From one side to another
He formed a bridge between two places
Where we can meet each other
And at the center of this bridge
We find eternity in the heart
And it is here
Where I will forever hold you
So that we will never part
For within the loving arms of Jesus
The distance between us
Has been completely measured
And it is through the heart
Where pure love is always treasured
And the distance once so far
Seems to fade away
Within a place, inside the heart
Where heaven meets earth each day

Do not follow where the path may lead, go instead where there is no path and leave a trail

—Ralph Waldo Emerson

Heavenly Messages~ Forever In My Heart® messages are a unique and inspirational brand of poems intended for your loved ones in heaven. When I began to write these messages several years ago, I didn't know how to use them or why I was writing them. I eventually became aware that God was expanding my heart and allowing me to see that when one suffers we all suffer together.

Since grief can be a very lonely and isolating experience it was a great awakening to learn that I was not alone. God taught me that the cry of one suffering heart can be felt by all. God was healing me message by message. Finally, I was able to see the work that was ahead of me and I accepted this path with honor. As the founder of Tuscan Vine Company, LLC, I create each message as outdoor cards that can be placed at a cemetery, in a garden, or any special site. I am committed to creating inspiring thoughts that serve as an expression of your love and strength through loss. In doing this work, I have met many beautiful, courageous, and inspirational people. The grieving heart is the purest heart to encounter.

Today, I see that every message that comes forth is like a miracle, almost like a birth. I never know what will be created or what the final result will look like, but I always know that the card will be beautiful and meaningful to someone, somewhere, and with that I am fulfilled. My work and mission are dedicated to the loving memory of all those who are no longer with us but through love, will always be forever in our hearts.

As an Emotional Intelligence Life Coach, spiritual teacher, and human being I understand the way negative emotions can affect our life. Yet, it is the divine polarity of these emotions that has the miraculous ability to offer balance and healing. Healing is the process of life. Throughout your life, and throughout healing, there will be times when you will feel close to God and times you will feel far from God. These waves of emotion are keeping you connected to the vast power of Source that continually flows into your being to heal and wash away the debris that has been trapped in your soul.

Your awareness of your emotions, thoughts, and feelings will guide you to your healing power. Your willingness to flow with this power will move you forward until it is time to go back to become aware again. Like a wave, you are continually pulled back and forth by various emotions in order to transfer any distorted or unholy energy that is flowing within your soul and align it with God. As you journey through healing, always be kind, loving and patient with yourself. As Thomas More said, "Our emotional symptoms are precious sources of life and individuality." Let your emotions serve as your guides to connect you to the healing power that God has individualized through you. Accepting your emotions, thoughts, and feelings allows you to move toward personal freedom within your life. Your emotions are the perfect expression of God's loving presence that is always beautifying your soul and healing your life.

The Messaging Process allows you to search within yourself in order to heal and transform your life. Messaging invites you to journey within to discover the loving presence of healing as it carries and holds you throughout every moment. Grief is a necessary part of the healing process from loss, but if you feel you are stuck in the darkness of grief, then Messaging is a process that can move you toward the light. When you turn inward to the sacred dwelling of truth, you encounter a transformative power that allows you to embrace an inner knowing of the divine. It is in this place that you become aware of this healing presence and your life meets its fullest potential to heal.

Healing can only be realized through introspection, self discovery, and purification of the soul. The healing that you desire desires you. Every moment of every day your healing potential waits within, but you are too busy trying to find it outside yourself. Most of us think it is somewhere in the future, waiting for our arrival. Yet healing is with you at this very moment. As you move toward the healing grace that

God has weaved within your inner life, you will encounter seeds of healing potential. Then, your true life will be introduced to itself. You will discover healing, fulfillment, and become fully awakened.

Your time to begin healing is here and now. Open the door and have the gift of healing that exists inside of you welcome you in. You can return to life again by transforming your pain and sorrow with truth and love. Your inner being desires to know you and heal you. The Messaging Process is your gateway to your soul's purest thoughts, deepest love, and the constant healing power of God.

I am thankful for the opportunity to share these messages and the Messaging Process with you. I know that writing these inspired words and creating this Messaging Process expanded my heart and healed my life. I believe they have the power to do the same for you. I hope these words and process serve with compassion and understanding. These words and this process are my embrace to you; they are my heart with love and my shoulder to lean on. Through loss we find ourselves here. Through missing links our souls are chained. It may be that some losses are greater than others; however, sorrow knows no measure. And yes, grief is a personal experience, but at times too personal and very isolating. You are not alone. I hold you in my heart and offer you my love, strength, and comfort. We need to reach, support, and connect with each other through our soulful chain. May the love and peace of God abide within you always.

With love, light, and peace,
Debra Ann

To God, my Divine Creator, I am deeply grateful for the inspiration and grace that has been given to me through the poems and the Messaging Process ... Let this sacred labor lead those who are so broken and hurt with sorrow to the Holy Encounter of your presence. Let the blessing of your wisdom be given to the hearts of your beloved by touching them with your love, compassion, comfort and profound healing. Amen.

Now it is your turn to Message a thank-you prayer note to God for your healing journey and the treasured gifts you have discovered about your life on the remaining portion of this page.

To God, my Divine Creator, I am deeply grateful for...

There will be times in life when we are challenged beyond our greatest capacity to endure. The loss of a loved one and grief are one of life's most challenging experiences. It is during this experience in life when we discover our true selves. We find that not only are we stronger than we can ever dream or imagine but we are infinite in our ability to create and sustain life through love and hope. We learn through our struggles that a greater power than us—Eternal Spirit, Universal Source, or God—is empowering us and directing our every step toward healing and restoration. We begin to travel the path less taken and discover that it is mapping our way to the hidden treasures that exist within all us yet would have never been found if we had not encountered the healing journey.

Thoughts and emotions have direct relationship to your quality of life, especially after loss. You have the power and ability to move through internal trappings of depression, sorrow and pain of grief with courage, hope and peace. This book will introduce you to a process called Messaging. The Messaging Process is a tool that allows you to dialogue and write through the negative thought patterns associated with grief and move you toward the truth of spirit that exist in your heart.

The Messaging Process will:

- Guide you through a fifteen-day process of writing and internal exploration as you begin the healing journey through grief
- Discover love and truth in the midst of grief
- Allow you to gain an understanding of your emotions and learn to recognize and appreciate these internal signals as messengers toward self empowerment and healing during grief
- Transform your life with personal freedom by replacing your negative emotions and feelings with divine wisdom and guidance
- Encourage you to gain a greater connection to spirit through visualization, affirmations, prayer and meditation

- Invite you to be willing to release your grief and allow the experience to be integrated into your life as you awaken and remember the sanctuary of your soul
- Allow you to understand and implement the power of creativity into your healing
- Most of all, the Messaging Process will return you to love, spirit and wholeness as you journey through grief on your spiritual path toward healing.

This book includes a collection of poetic messages called Heavenly Messages~ Forever In My Heart®. These messages were specially written and created for those who have experienced the loss of a loved one.

Debra Ann holds a Master of Science Degree from St. John's University School of Education and Human Services, New York. She is the author of Heavenly Messages~ Forever In My Heart® messages, a unique brand of spiritual eternity cards. As a Certified Emotional Intelligence (EI) Life Coach and Spiritual Teacher, her greatest desire is to elevate the power of healing through self awareness and soul exploration. She hopes to unify healing by offering a process that allows you to fully integrate the experience of grief in a healthy, loving, and honorable way.

If you are interested in having a Heavenly Message~ Forever In My Heart® eternity card created for you, if you would like support with the Messaging Process as a spiritual tool toward healing your life, or if you have a poem you would like to share, please feel free to contact her at TuscanVine@aol.com or you can visit the website at www.tuscanvinecompany.com.